your visit to VERSAILLES

Editorial co-ordination: Denis Kilian (Director, Éditions Art Lys)
Editorial follow-up and picture research: Christian Ryo
Graphic design and layout: Martine Mène
Plans: Thierry Lebreton, Dominique Bissière
Production: Pierre Kegels

ISBN 2-85495-135-2

your visit to VERSAILLES

SIMONE HOOG

Honorary Curator of the Estate

BÉATRIX SAULE

Head Curator
at the Château of Versailles

art lys ♩

CONTENTS

VERSAILLES

Louis XIII
(1601-1643)

Anne of Austria
(1601-1666)

Louis XIV
(1638-1715)

Maria-Theresa
of Spain
(1638-1683)

Louis, Dauphin
(1661-1711)

Louis-François
(1672-1672)

Philippe-
Charles
(1668-1671)

Marie-Thérèse
(1667-1672)

Marie-Anne
(1664-1664)

Anne-Elisabeth
(1662-1662)

Louis, duc
de Bourgogne
(1682-1712)

Philippe,
duc d'Anjou,
became Philip
V of Spain in
1700
(1683-1746)

Charles,
duc de Berry
(1686-1714)

1624
Louis XIII has
a hunting-lodge
built at Versailles.

1631
Louis XIII asks
Philibert Le Roy to build
a château on the site
of the hunting-lodge.

1643
Louis XIII stays at Versailles
for the last time.

1660
Marriage of Louis XIV
to Maria-Theresa of Spain.
The King brings his wife
to Versailles on October 25.

1664
Festivities
of *Les Plaisirs de l'île enchantée.*

1668
Grand Divertissement
at Versailles.

1682
Louis XIV declares Versailles
the official residence of the
Court and seat of government.

1684
Completion
of the Hall of Mirrors.

1710
Consecration
of the Royal Chapel on June 5.

1715
September 1, death of Louis XIV.
September 9, Louis XV abandons
Versailles for Vincennes.

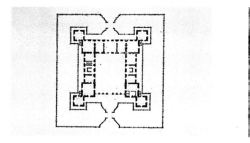

Louis XIII's "little château"

The Château of Versailles in 1668
by Pierre Patel

The colonnade (construction started in 1685)
by Jules Hardouin-Mansart

ENGLAND AND THE USA

1625
Charles I is proclaimed king
of England.

1649
Charles I is beheaded.

1653
Oliver Cromwell
is proclaimed Lord Protector.

1658
Death of Cromwell.
The Monarchy is restored.

1660
Charles II, raised
to the Court of Louis XIV,
rises to the throne

1666
Fire of London.

1682
The Sieur de la Salle founds
Louisiana.

1688
James II escapes to France.

1713
Treaty of Utrecht, Spanish
possessions are divided:
Philip V, grandson of Louis XIV,
keeps Spain and its colonies,
Britain gains Gibraltar, Minorca,
Newfoundland, Nova Scotia,
and the Hudson Bay territories.

1714-1727
Reign of George I.

Louis XV
(1710-1774)

Maria Leczinska
(1703-1768)

1722
Louis XV returns to live
at Versailles.

1736
September 26, opening
of the Hercules Drawing-Room.

1757
Attempt on Louis XV's
life by Damiens.

1768
The Petit Trianon
is completed.

1774
May 10, Louis XV dies of
smallpox at Versailles.

Louis Dauphin
(1729-1765)

Philippe-Louis
(1730-1733)

Adélaïde
(1732-1800)

Victoire
(1733-1799)

Sophie
(1734-1782)

Thérèse-Félicité
(1736-1744)

Louise
(1737-1787)

Louis XVI
(1754-1793)

Marie-Antoinette
of Austria-Lorraine
(1755-1793)

1777
Visit of Joseph II, Emperor
of Austria, the Queen's brother.

1783
Signing of the Treaty
of Versailles, acknowledging
the independence
of the United States of America.

1783-1786
Construction
of the Queen's Hamlet.

1789
May 5, opening of the States
General. October 6, the King,
the Royal Family and the Court
leave Versailles for good.

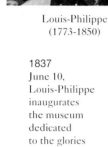

Louis-Philippe
(1773-1850)

1837
June 10,
Louis-Philippe
inaugurates
the museum
dedicated
to the glories
of France.

Château of Versailles in 1722
by Pierre-Denis Martin

Illumination of the Belvedere in honour of Joseph II
by Claude-Louis Chatelet

Inauguration of the Hall of Battles
by Jean-Augusta Bard

1714-1727
Reign of George I.

1727-1760
Reign of George II.

1760-1820
Reign of George III.

1775-1783
The uprising in the American
colonies leads to recognition
of the United States

1777
The French General Lafayette
comes to fight alongside
the American insurgents.

1787
September 17,
United States Constitution.

1788
Creation of *The Times*.

1789
George Washington elected
President of the United States
of America.

1837
Queen Victoria
rises to the throne.

WALKS IN THE GARDENS

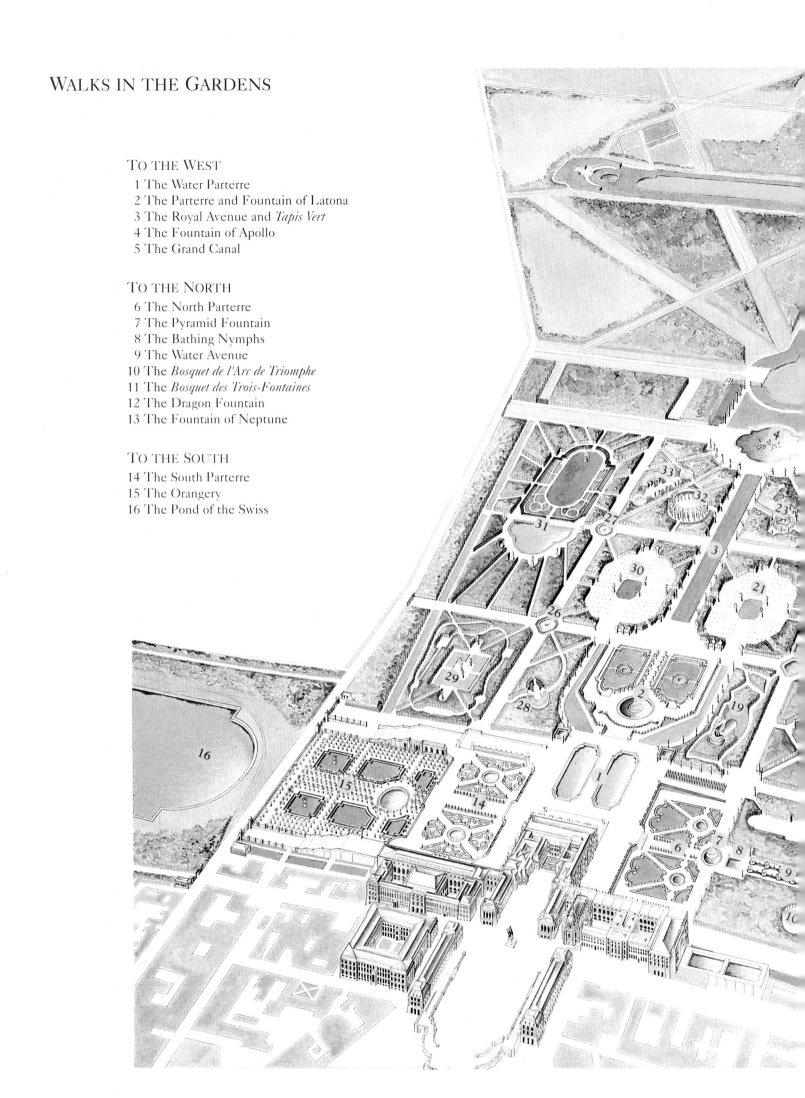

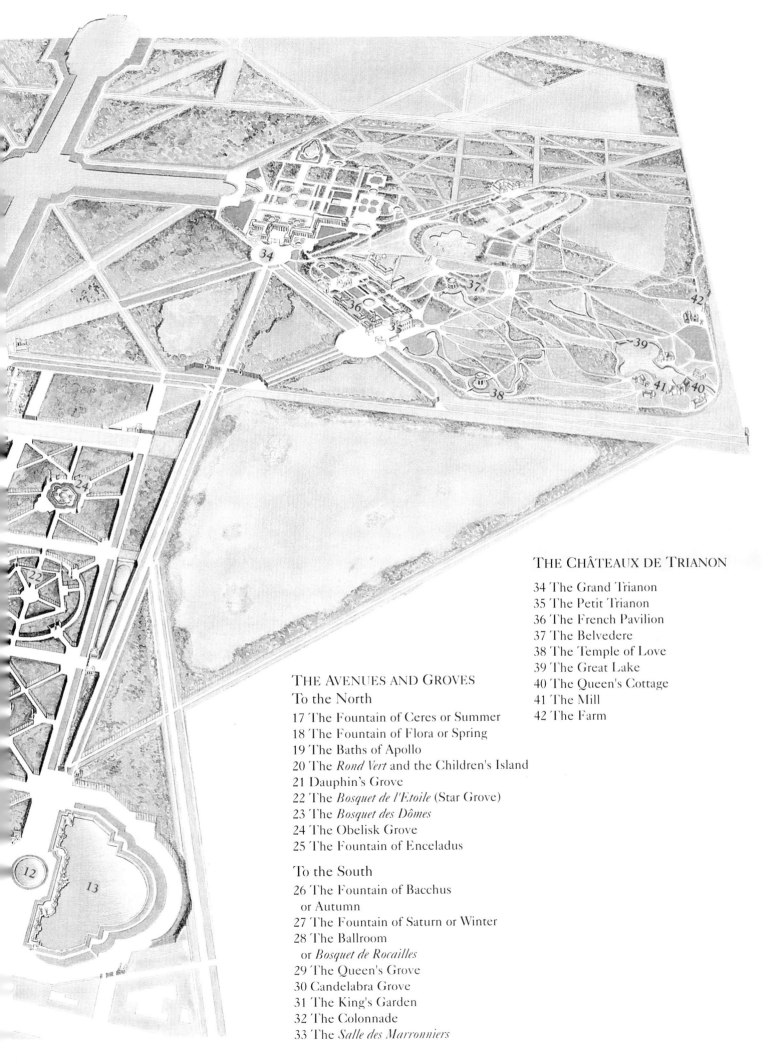

THE CHÂTEAUX DE TRIANON

34 The Grand Trianon
35 The Petit Trianon
36 The French Pavilion
37 The Belvedere
38 The Temple of Love
39 The Great Lake
40 The Queen's Cottage
41 The Mill
42 The Farm

THE AVENUES AND GROVES

To the North

17 The Fountain of Ceres or Summer
18 The Fountain of Flora or Spring
19 The Baths of Apollo
20 The *Rond Vert* and the Children's Island
21 Dauphin's Grove
22 The *Bosquet de l'Etoile* (Star Grove)
23 The *Bosquet des Dômes*
24 The Obelisk Grove
25 The Fountain of Enceladus

To the South

26 The Fountain of Bacchus
 or Autumn
27 The Fountain of Saturn or Winter
28 The Ballroom
 or *Bosquet de Rocailles*
29 The Queen's Grove
30 Candelabra Grove
31 The King's Garden
32 The Colonnade
33 The *Salle des Marronniers*

TOUR OF THE KING'S BEDCHAMBER

The Dauphin's Apartment

1 The Guardroom
2 The First Antechamber
3 The Second Antechamber
4 The Bedchamber
5 The State Cabinet
6 The Library

The Dauphine's Apartment

7 The Private Cabinet
8 The Bedchamber
9 The State Chamber
10 The Second Antechamber
11 The First Antechamber

THE OTHER TOURS

Madame Victoire's Apartment

12 The First Antechamber
13 The *Salon des Nobles*
14 The State Cabinet
15 The Bedchamber
16 The Private Cabinet
17 The Library

Madame Adélaïde's Apartment

18 The Private Cabinet
19 The Bedchamber
20 The State Cabinet

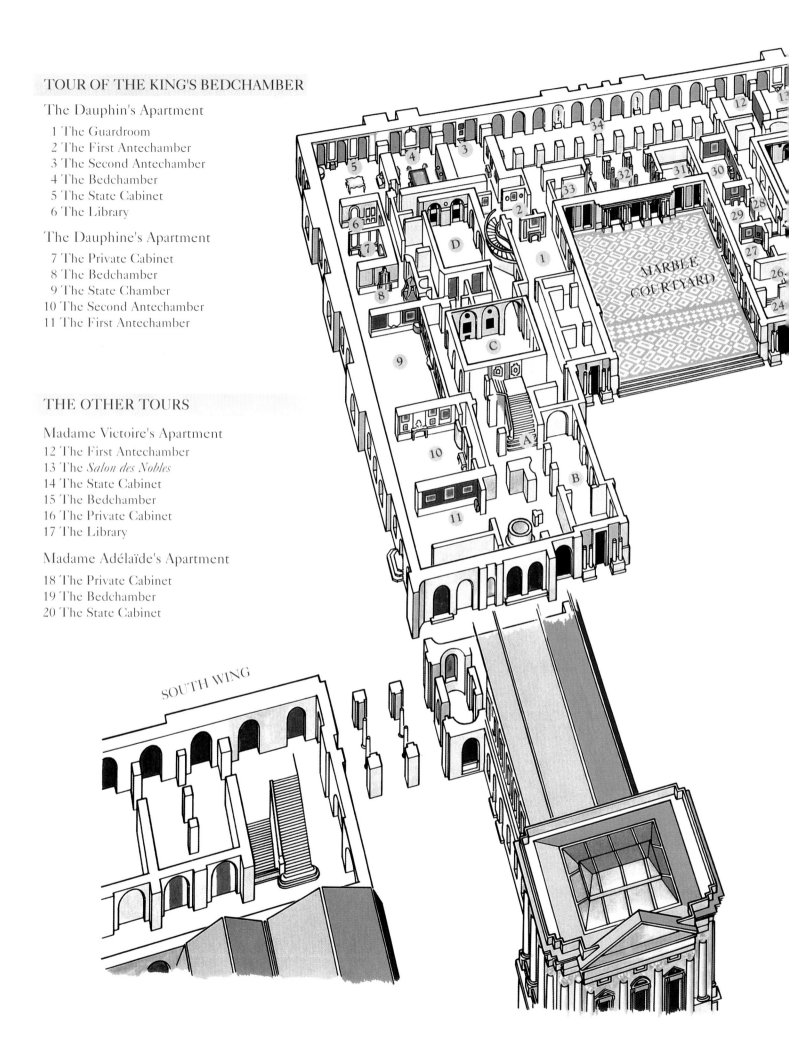

MARBLE COURTYARD

SOUTH WING

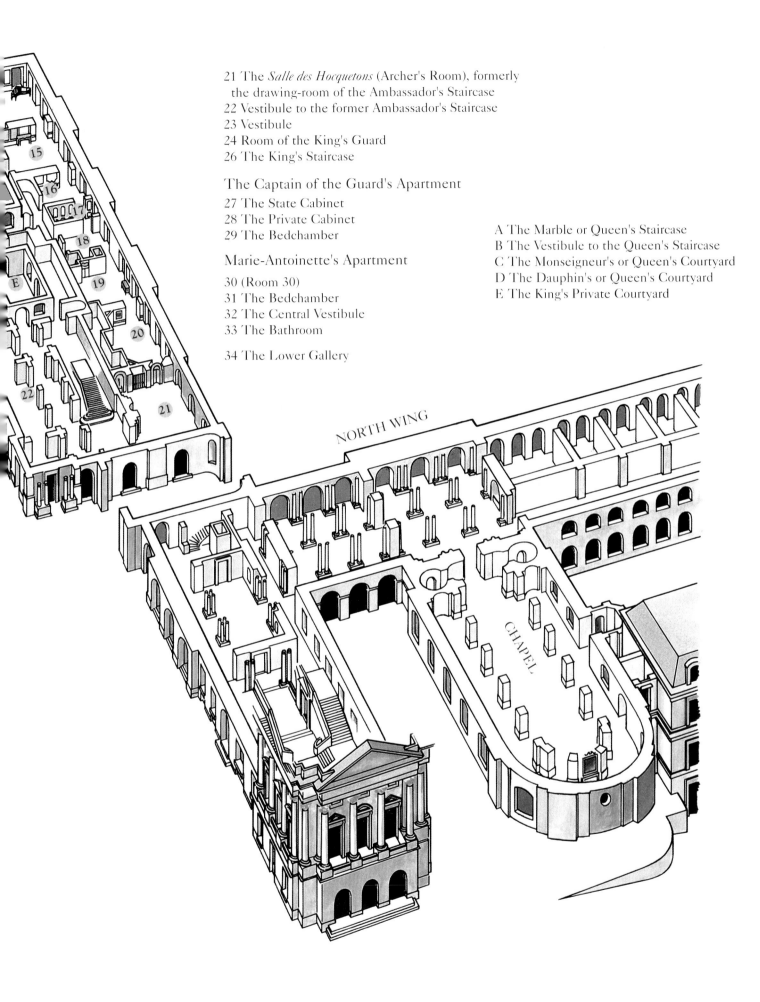

21 The *Salle des Hocquetons* (Archer's Room), formerly
  the drawing-room of the Ambassador's Staircase
22 Vestibule to the former Ambassador's Staircase
23 Vestibule
24 Room of the King's Guard
26 The King's Staircase

The Captain of the Guard's Apartment
27 The State Cabinet
28 The Private Cabinet
29 The Bedchamber

Marie-Antoinette's Apartment
30 (Room 30)
31 The Bedchamber
32 The Central Vestibule
33 The Bathroom

34 The Lower Gallery

A The Marble or Queen's Staircase
B The Vestibule to the Queen's Staircase
C The Monseigneur's or Queen's Courtyard
D The Dauphin's or Queen's Courtyard
E The King's Private Courtyard

NORTH WING

CHAPEL

TOUR OF THE STATE APARTMENTS

The State Apartment

1 The Drawing-Room of Plenty
2 The Venus Drawing-Room
3 The Diana Drawing-Room
4 The Mars Drawing-Room
5 The Mercury Drawing-Room
6 The Apollo Drawing-Room
7 The War Drawing-Room
8 The Peace Drawing-Room

The Queen's Apartment

9 The Queen's Bedchamber
10 The State Cabinet or *Salon des Nobles*
11 The Antechamber of the *Grand Couvert*
12 The Guardroom

THE OTHER TOURS

The Queen's Private Rooms

a The Annexe to the Library
b The Private Cabinet
c The Library
d The Meridian Cabinet
e The Duchesse de Bourgogne's Cabinet

Madame de Maintenon's Apartment

g-h Antechambers
i The Bedchamber
j The State Cabinet

TOUR OF THE KING'S BEDCHAMBER

The King's Apartment

13 The Marble (or Queen's) Staircase
14 The Loggia (also leading to the King's Apartment)
15 The Guardroom
16 The Antechamber of the *Grand Couvert*
17 The Antechamber of the *Œuil-de-Boeuf*
18 The King's Bedchamber
19 The Council Chamber

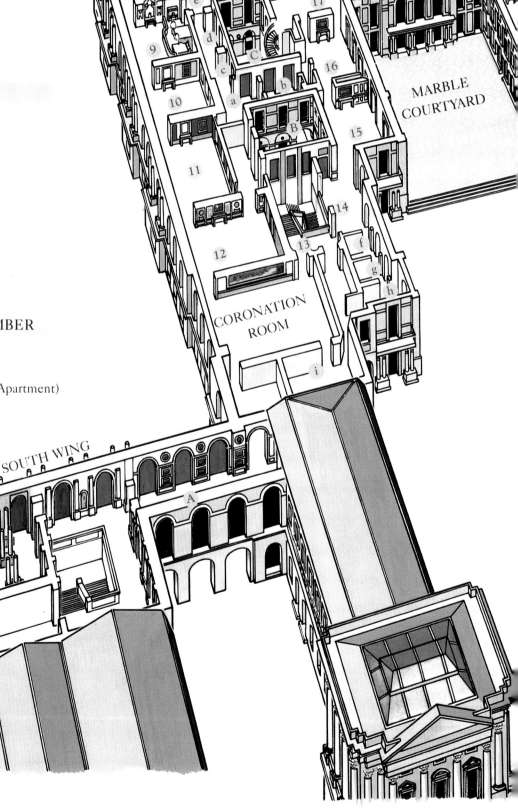

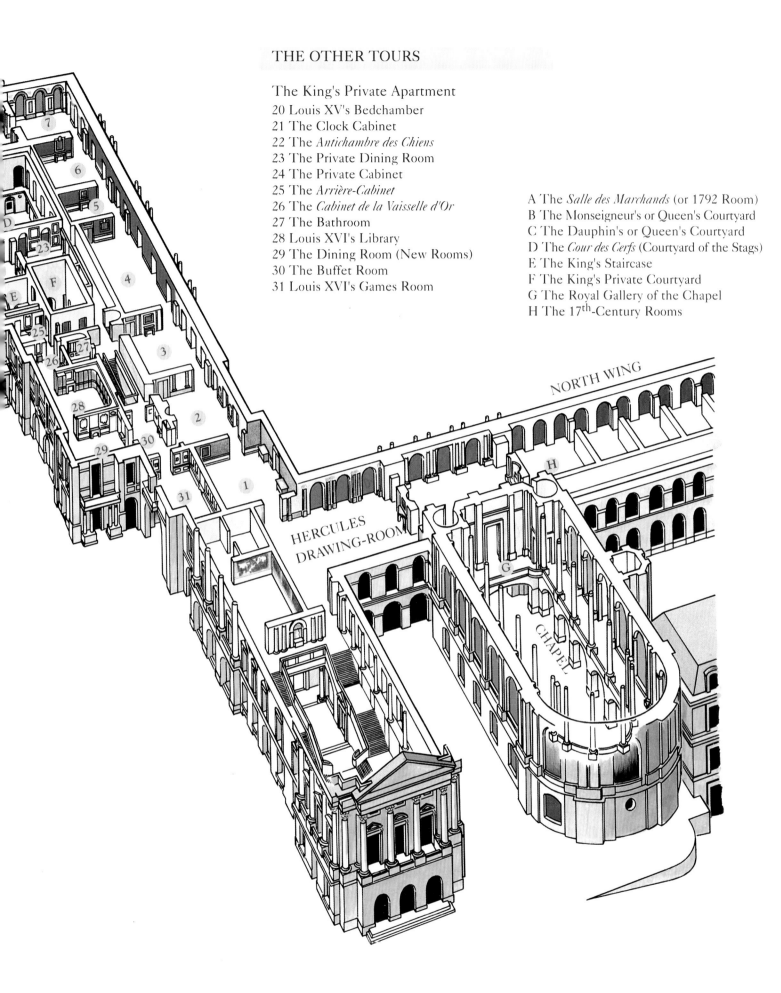

THE OTHER TOURS

The King's Private Apartment
20 Louis XV's Bedchamber
21 The Clock Cabinet
22 The *Antichambre des Chiens*
23 The Private Dining Room
24 The Private Cabinet
25 The *Arrière-Cabinet*
26 The *Cabinet de la Vaisselle d'Or*
27 The Bathroom
28 Louis XVI's Library
29 The Dining Room (New Rooms)
30 The Buffet Room
31 Louis XVI's Games Room

A The *Salle des Marchands* (or 1792 Room)
B The Monseigneur's or Queen's Courtyard
C The Dauphin's or Queen's Courtyard
D The *Cour des Cerfs* (Courtyard of the Stags)
E The King's Staircase
F The King's Private Courtyard
G The Royal Gallery of the Chapel
H The 17th-Century Rooms

NORTH WING

HERCULES DRAWING-ROOM

CHAPEL

VERSAILLES,
SEAT OF THE ANCIENT MONARCHY

Although Louis XIII had a hunting-lodge and garden built there in the 1630s, Louis XIV was mainly responsible for the creation of Versailles. Not too close to Paris, where insurgency was a constant threat, but not too far away, the site had great potential for building. It thus fulfilled the King's desire to have his court permanently around him, which no other royal residence in the surrounding areas permitted. He turned Versailles into a sumptuous estate and ensured its destiny. From 1682 to 1789, Versailles was the seat and later the symbol of absolute monarchy, since the estate, modelled according to the Sun King's wishes, reflected his perception of power.

THE SEAT OF POWER

In an absolute monarchy, all power comes from the King. At Versailles, Louis XIV was both the host and ruler of the kingdom which he governed through various intermediaries who were completely indebted to him. Distracted from their business, those in high places no longer exercised real power, but nevertheless felt the need to appear at court. It was there that the king would dispense favours: offices, land, titles, and pensions etc. This society based on prestige and representation demanded constant rivalry, compulsory luxury and extravagant living. This was how Louis XIV "kept" his courtiers. He himself had to hold sway in everything. In his eyes, the exercise and manifestation of power were one and the same. His dwelling had to be the largest and the most magnificent, its décor filled with symbols pertaining to his glory. The staff of servants, in the noblest sense, in the King's household had to be the largest and his court much frequented: on different days, there would be 3000 to 10,000 persons at court. This sizeable crowd called for strict regulations. Etiquette and its irksome aspects - who has access to the king, who has the right to sit in his presence, who ranks above who, etc. - may appear trivial today. However, this system was essential since it asserted the different ranks, the primacy of the King, in a word: the hierarchy within the court. It applied to the sovereign's most intimate moments - rising, retiring, meals and walks - which were perceived as state activities seemed to revolve around the King's personal existence. Another distinctive characteristic of Versailles, which quite rightly surprised outsiders, was the fact that the gardens and the château interiors were largely open to the public. Without necessarily being part of the court, anyone was able to see the King as he passed through his State Apartment on his way to the chapel; anyone had access right up to his bedchamber, but only in his absence. All the functions relating to representation, government, living, and service account for the layout of the different areas. However, all this was not created in a day.

FIFTY YEARS OF BUILDING WORK

When, at the start of his personal reign in 1661, Louis XIV went to his father's château to amuse himself and order the first alterations, he did not imagine that this small edifice, which consisted of the buildings surrounding the Marble Courtyard, would become the heart of such an immense estate. During this period of youth, the gardens, immediately entrusted to Le Nôtre, were the setting for extraordinary festivities which brought Versailles renown throughout Europe. It was the day after the *Grand Divertissement* in 1668 that the King first decided to extend the château. Le Vau and d'Orbay, architects to the King, surrounded the original château with three main buildings overlooking the park. The new constructions, made of stone and in the style of Roman baroque villas popular at the time, contrasted so greatly with the brick, stone and slate architecture dating from Louis XIII that they could almost be two different châteaux built into each other. Le Brun, chief painter to the King, provided the designs for the entire interior decoration of the State Apartments and the sculptural décor of the fountains with their multiple water effects in the parterres, avenues and groves. Apollo, the sun god, with whom the King was identified, was the prevailing theme.

In 1677, Louis XIV announced his decision to establish the court and government permanently at Versailles. Immense work was then initiated which, despite the tens of thousands of labourers employed, was far from completion when the monarchy was finally established there in 1682. Under the supervision of J. Hardouin-Mansart, the constructed areas increased fivefold with the addition of the two stables, the *Grand Commun*, the south and north wings and the Grand Trianon. The Hall of Mirrors replaced the central terrace on the first floor. The interiors were repeatedly rearranged, the groves constantly reworked, and increasingly ambitious plans for laying on water undertaken. However, the wars at the end of the reign held up the different projects. The chapel was only completed in 1710. Through the sheer determination of the King, fifty years of effort, hesitation, trials and tribulations finally led to the creation of an estate in which everything was mastered - both man and nature, where everything was ordered around an axis passing through the very centre of the royal residence which since 1701 had marked the site of the King's Bedchamber.

SEEMINGLY, NOTHING HAD CHANGED

The death of Louis XIV in 1715 did not lead to the disappearance of the court "mechanism" which had become an attribute of royalty and continued to govern the life of Versailles. Until 1789, it imposed itself on Louis XV followed by Louis XVI who were obliged to go through the same motions in the same places as their grandfather. Despite being considered increasingly restricting, costly and outdated, no reforms could be made without affecting too many privileges. Versailles therefore continued to function as in the time of the Great King, or seemingly at least. Unlike Louis XVI who was not a great builder, Louis XV put the finishing touches to the work of his great-grandfather in the same spirit of magnificence through the decoration of the Hercules Drawing- Room, the Fountain of Neptune and the Opera.

However, alongside this official existence, the sovereigns made a simple private life for themselves which spared them the constraints of etiquette. Elegance and privacy were the key principles. Private apartments and cabinets multiplied within the château, accommodating very restricted circles of friends in décor constantly changing with the fashion. The greatest refinements of décor, conversation, music and gastronomy were expressed there, in every detail.

Kings and queens would withdraw all too often to their private apartments or to Trianon. Louis XV and even more so Marie-Antoinette adopted this attitude without foreseeing the consequences. The courtiers grew weary: there was little point in coming to Versailles. On the eve of the Revolution, the court was deserted, the nobility estranged from the King.

FROM THE REVOLUTION TO THE PRESENT DAY

The Revolution stripped the château of its furniture, but spared the building itself. After years of near negligence, it was restored first by Napoleon I, then by King Louis XVIII and Charles X, both brothers of Louis XVI. But no-one dared reign at Versailles; to establish oneself there would certainly be perceived as provocation, signifying the return of the *Ancien Régime* and all its privileges. When the future of the Versailles became uncertain and there was even thought of destroying the château, it was saved by Louis-Philippe. In a spirit of national reconciliation, the "King of the French" transformed it into a "museum dedicated to the glories of France." Inaugurated in 1837, the historical galleries constitute a monumental summary of French history, from the creation of the kingdom to the modern era.

Alongside the history museum, curators and architects have been working since the beginning of the 20th century to restore and re-furnish the royal apartments at heart of the château, while enriching the collections of paintings and sculptures which still occupy the wings.

Three centuries after its creation and despite having lost its hunting grounds, the estate is still vast with its three châteaux, gardens, park and outbuildings: surface area of 800 hectares, 20 km of roads and as many enclosing walls, 200,000 trees and even more flowers planted each year, 35 km of pipes, 11 hectares of roofing, 2153 windows, and 67 staircases...

THE COACH MUSEUM

The Coach Museum is located in the Great Stables, built by J. Hardouin-Mansart in 1680. It occupies a gallery which has preserved its original appearance, its oak wainscoting with the fodder racks and its elegant wrought iron lanterns. The carriages on display were amassed by Louis-Philippe. This is how the berlins of the wedding of Napoleon I came to Versailles, seven gala carriages reminiscent of the magnificence of the Imperial Court at its pinnacle, on 2 April 1810. This was also the case for the Coronation Coach of Charles X, designed by Percier, architect to Louis XVIII who did not, however, dare use the carriage in the political context of the recent Restoration. Louis-Philippe also acquired sedan chairs and sleighs. These were already in existence at Versailles during the *Ancien Régime*, and were used for races through the snow-covered avenues of the park or on the frozen Grand Canal. In 1833, the funeral carriage of Louis XVIII joined the collection, and is the only example of a royal hearse to have been preserved.

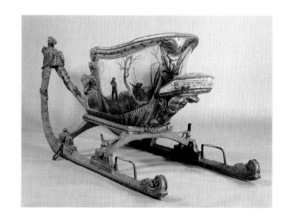

Sleigh with "skater", France, circa 1730,
Former Royal Collection

The funeral carriage of Louis XVIII.
Design: Lecointe and Hittorff, Architects;
body and axles: Daldringen,
Saddler-Coach Builder to the King;
sculptures: Roguier, Sculptor;
trimming: Renault, Master Upholsterer

THE COURTYARDS
AND FAÇADES,
TOWN SIDE

Three avenues (the Avenue de Saint-Cloud, the Avenue de Paris, and the Avenue de Sceaux), bordering the Great Stables and the Small Stables, converge onto the *Place d'Armes*, thus named since this was where the royal army carried out its military exercises. Behind the gateway, surmounted by the Royal Arms of France, there is a succession of three narrowing courtyards: the Great Courtyard, the Royal Courtyard (closed during the *Ancien Régime* by a second gateway where the statue of Louis XIV, erected in 1837, now stands), and the Marble Courtyard. The *"Petit Château"*, with the slate roof and brick and stone façades, built by Louis XIII and preserved by Louis XIV, overlooks the Marble Courtyard.

Several plans for reworking the façades were devised in the latter half of the 18th century, including the pavilion built by the architect Gabriel on the northern side of the Royal Courtyard.

*The gateway
surmounted by
the Royal Arms
of France*

TOUR OF THE STATE APARTMENTS

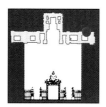

THE HISTORICAL GALLERIES

Louis-Philippe, King of the French from 1830 to 1848, desired to reconcile the partisans of the different regimes following on from each other since 1789. By inaugurating the museum "dedicated to the glories of France", in 1837, he made Versailles a symbol of the monarchy of the *Ancien Régime*, a place devoted to the memory of the entire history of France. This involved depicting the great figures which had established the French nation, from Clovis, Napoleon I and Louis XIV to himself. He transformed the apartments of the princes and courtiers, situated in the north and south wings, into vast galleries displaying paintings and sculptures contemporary with the events and figures portrayed, or commissioned by artists in vogue at the time.

THE CRUSADES GALLERIES

The epic of the eight Crusades which took place from the 11th to the 13th century, presented here, is portrayed as perceived by the romanticists, in a neo-Gothic setting characteristic of the medieval tastes of the first half of the 19th century. The ceilings are adorned with the coats of arms of the families who became renowned during the expeditions to the Middle East. The cedarwood doors and bronze mortar originating from the Hospital of the Knights of Saint John of Jerusalem in Rhodes, situated in the largest of the five rooms, were given to Louis-Philippe, in 1836, by Sultan Mahmoud.

Bohemond I,
Prince of Antioch,
by Merry-Joseph Blondel

THE SEVENTEENTH-CENTURY GALLERIES

These galleries, situated in the north wing, are devoted to 17th-century iconography in the programme for the Museum of the History of France, created by Louis-Philippe. They therefore serve as an introduction to the tour of the apartments since they portray the figures and events contemporary with the building of Versailles or related to the genealogy of the Bourbons.

The reign of Louis XIV is clearly the predominant feature, with works illustrating the life of the Court, the craftsmen and senior civil servants, together with the talented artists with which the Monarch surrounded himself. Certain paintings, such as that by Henri Testelin showing Colbert presenting the members of the Royal Academy of Science, created in 1666, to Louis XIV (following page), bear witness to the Sovereign's interest in the development of science.

Above:
Jean-Baptiste Colbert
(1619-1683),
Controller General
of Finances,
by Claude Lefèvre

Right:
André Le Nôtre
(1613-1700),
Controller General
of the King's Gardens,
by Carlo Maratta

MEMOIRS OF THE COMTESSE DE BOIGNE

"I was invited to the inauguration of Versailles [in 1837]. I do not believe that it would be possible to invent something more magnificent than the material of the festivities; it was indeed worthy of the surroundings, which is quite enough praise. The company gathered there seemed fairly mixed. It was the Palace of Louis XIV invaded by the bourgeoisie. There was an abundance of journalists, bringing with them the conceit which follows them everywhere, and which they displayed within these surroundings where they themselves perhaps felt somewhat out of place. The King was sitting beneath the painting in the gallery where it is written in large gilded letters: "The King rules alone." As it was precisely the beginning of lengthy debates on the text of *The King Reigns But Does Not Rule*, we were convinced that this incident would not pass without comment."

Henri de la Tour d'Auvergne,
Vicomte de Turenne, Maréchal de France,
by Charles Le Brun

Top:
The Château and Gardens of Versailles
in 1668, by Pierre Patel

Left page:
Colbert presenting the members of the Royal
Academy of Science, created in 1666,
to Louis XIV (detail), by Henri Testelin

THE ROYAL CHAPEL

Completed in 1710, only five years before the death of Louis XIV, the Royal Chapel is the Château's fifth chapel, but the first to occupy a separate building. Hardouin-Mansart's plans were approved in 1699, and after his death in 1708, the work was taken over by his brother-in-law Robert de Cotte. Dedicated to Saint Louis, it follows the tradition of the Palatine chapels, with a ground floor for the public and "officials", and a floor reserved for the Sovereign and the royal family. The King would hear Mass from the gallery connected to the State Apartment on the same floor. Each morning, in order to attend prayers, the King would leave his Bedchamber, go through the Hall of Mirrors, then cross the state drawing-rooms and the upper chapel vestibule. This was an important event in the daily life of the Court. It was in this very chapel that the ceremonies of the Order of the Holy Spirit, and the baptisms and weddings of the Children of France took place between 1710 and 1789.

Towering above the altar, opposite the Royal Gallery, are the Robert Cliquot organs (1707-1711) (restored and inaugurated in 1995), which François Couperin Le Grand often had the privilege to play.

PRINCESS PALATINE,
VERSAILLES,
20 FEBRUARY 1695

"It is a great honour to be seated next to the King during the sermon, but I would gladly surrender my place as H.M. will not allow me to rest; as soon as I fall asleep, the King nudges my elbow and wakes me up."

The Deposition from the Cross, gilded bronze bas-relief on the high altar, by Corneille van Clève

SAINT SIMON, MEMOIRS

"The King attended Mass, where
his musicians always sang
a motet. He went downstairs
only for major festivities,
or for ceremonies. On the way
to or from Mass, anyone could
talk to him if he wished,
but less distinguished persons
had to clear the Captain
of the Guards first, and he went
there and back by the door
of the Cabinets in the Hall.
During Mass, the ministers were
notified, and they assembled
in the King's chamber,
where dignitaries could meet
them and talk. The King had
little time for amusement
after Mass, and almost always
convened the Council
straightaway. And that completed
the morning."

*Central part
of the chapel vault:
The Heavenly Father in His Glory
Announcing to the World the Promise
of Redemption, by Antoine Coypel*

THE STATE APARTMENT

The State Apartment overlooks the gardens to the north, and occupies the extension built by Hardouin-Mansart. This was the setting for the public life of the King, whereas his private existence was reserved for the Private Apartments (also called the Private Cabinets in the 18th century) overlooking the courtyards. The State Apartment therefore served as a ceremonial apartment and as reception rooms, particularly during "apartment evenings", on Monday, Wednesday and Thursday evenings: "apartment evenings was the name used to describe the meeting of the entire Court, from seven o'clock in the evening to ten o'clock when the King would sit down at the table, in the State Apartment, from one of the drawing-rooms at the end of the Great Hall [Hall of Mirrors] up to the gallery of the Royal Chapel." (Saint Simon)

THE HERCULES DRAWING-ROOM

Having been used as a chapel while the present chapel, completed in 1710, was being built, work was carried out on this site over a long period of time. The décor, begun in 1712 with the installation of Veronese's monumental painting: *The Meal at the House of Simon*, painted for the Refectory of the Convent of the Servites in Venice in approximately 1570, and given to Louis XIV by the Republic of Venice in 1664, was interrupted by the death of the Sun King in 1715, and only resumed in 1725. Inspired by Veronese's colour and harmony, François Lemoine composed the ceiling representing *The Apotheosis of Hercules*, on which he had also hoped to portray *"Virtue Raising Man above Himself"*. This magnificent masterpiece consisting of 142 figures roused the enthusiasm of Louis XV. Despite this success and exhausted by the immense work, the artist committed suicide shortly afterwards.

Above the fireplace:
Eliezer and Rebecca, by Paul Veronese

THE DRAWING-ROOM OF PLENTY

The end door of this drawing-room originally opened onto the Cabinet of Curios and Rare Objects of Louis XIV (subsequently Louis XVI's Games Room). The King's collections of precious and rare objects, including the famous royal nef (depicted on the balustrade painted above the door), inspired the décor of the ceiling painted by René-Antoine Houasse under the supervision of Charles Le Brun. During "apartment evenings", buffet tables would be arranged there for refreshments.

Figure of Asia, by R.-A. Houasse

THE VENUS DRAWING-ROOM

This and the following room were reached by the famous Ambassadors' Staircase (demolished in 1752). This room was therefore the main entrance to the State Apartment and also the most luxurious with its marble columns and pilasters, its *trompe-l'oeil* perspectives which extend the architecture of the room, painted by Jacques Rousseau who also executed the two *trompe-l'oeil* statues of Meleager and Atalanta between the windows. The theme of the ceiling, painted by R.-A. Houasse, is *Venus Subjugating the Gods and Powers*. The coving is decorated with four paintings on bas-reliefs painted in monochrome: to the left, adjacent to the Drawing-Room of Plenty: *Augustus Presiding over the Circus Games* (referring to the 1662 carousel celebrations); opposite the windows: *Nebuchadnezzar and Semiramis and the Creation of the Hanging Gardens of Babylon* (referring to the work undertaken for the Royal Estate); adjacent to the Diana Drawing-Room: *Alexander's Marriage to Roxana* (referring to the wedding of Louis XIV); adjacent to the windows: *Cyrus Taking Arms to Rescue a Princess* (referring to the war of 1667). The statue of Louis XIV, the work of Jean Warin, bequeathed to the King by the sculptor in 1672, is situated in the alcove between the two doors at the far end of the room.

MERCURE GALANT,
DECEMBER 1682

"Since this drawing-room is used to serve the light supper, several well-laid tables line the walls. These tables are covered with silver candlesticks and round, long and square filigree baskets. They are filled with pyramids of fresh fruit, lemons, oranges, all types of dried and jellied fruits, and flowers."

Venus Subjugating the Gods and Powers, by R.-A. Houasse

THE DIANA DRAWING-ROOM

The Diana Drawing-Room, also reached by the Ambassadors' Staircase, therefore served as a vestibule to the State Apartment and, in the time of Louis XIV, as a billiards room during "apartment evenings". Two platforms were reserved for the ladies who wished to watch the game in which the King had been a past master. The central part of the ceiling, painted by Gabriel Blanchard, depicts *Diana in Her Chariot Presiding Over Hunting and Navigation*. The painting by Charles de Lafosse depicting *The Sacrifice of Iphigenia* has been returned to its original position above the fireplace; and opposite, above the console is *Diana Watching over the Sleeping Endymion* by Gabriel Blanchard. The antique busts are from the Mazarin collections bequeathed to Louis XIV.

*The bust of Louis XIV aged 27,
placed against the far wall, was executed
by Bernini from life in 1665*

PRINCESS PALATINE, VERSAILLES,
4 JANUARY 1699

"A great debate is underway at court,
and everyone from the King down
to the lackeys is taking sides.
It was Mr Fagon who raised the question;
the Cardinal d'Estrées, Abbé de Vaubran
and a few others are on his side;
the rest of the court has another opinion.
Here is the object of the dispute:
does the century start in the year 1700
or in the year 1701?
Mr Fagon and his party think it should
be 1700, because, according to them,
one hundred years have passed;
but the others argue that the century
is only over in the year 1701.
I would be interested in knowing
Mr Leibnitz' opinion on this matter.
Wherever you go nowadays,
you hear people discussing it;
even the porters are talking about it [...]"

THE MARS DRAWING-ROOM

Until 1684, this drawing-room was used as a guardroom, which explains the military-inspired décor. It was subsequently used for music and games during the "apartment evenings". The musicians sat in the two marble galleries, removed in 1750, on either side of the fireplace. The King, who was not averse to games, mingled with his courtiers and would sometimes stand in for one of them. In the centre of the ceiling, Claude Audran painted *Mars in a Chariot Drawn by Wolves*. The painting is flanked by two compositions, one to the east, by Jouvenet: *Victory Supported by Hercules Followed by Plenty and Felicity;* and the other, to the west, by Houasse: *Terror, Fury and Horror Seizing the Earthly Powers.* Four paintings by Simon Vouet, originating from the Château of Saint-Germain-en-Laye are situated above the doors: *Temperance, Prudence, Justice* and *Strength.* Domenichino's *King David Playing the Harp,* above the fireplace, decorated the alcove of the King's Bedchamber during the reign of Louis XIV, and was the counterpart of *Saint John*

on Patmos, then attributed to Raphael. *Darius and His Family at the Feet of Alexander* by Charles Le Brun can be seen to the left of the fireplace and, to the right, *The Pilgrims of Emmaus* in the style of Veronese. Two state portraits of Louis XV and Maria Leczinska, both by C. van Loo, hang on the side walls.

Décor of the northern coving: "Young children taking up arms and training in the exercises of war", by Claude Audran

THE MERCURY DRAWING-ROOM

Also known as the Bedchamber, the Mercury Drawing-Room was the State Bedchamber of the State Apartments. The state bed, hung with gold and silver brocade to match the walls, was closed off by a silver balustrade upon which stood eight candelabras. This precious furniture was melted down by order of the King himself in order to meet the expenses of war. The bed currently on display was commissioned by Louis-Philippe for the King's Bedchamber when Versailles was turned into a museum. Only the famous automaton clock, presented to Louis XIV by the designer Antoine Morand in 1706, has been returned to the place it originally occupied until the Revolution.

The Duc d'Anjou, grandson of Louis XIV, who became King of Spain in 1700, slept in this room for three weeks until he left for his new country. It was also in this room that the mortal remains of Louis XIV lay in state from 2 to 10 September 1715, while 72 priests took turns celebrating mass in the bedchamber, and the King's musicians sung *De Profundis*, the *Miserere* and the *Requiem* in the Mars Drawing-Room.

Henry de Favannes and Guy Vernansal executed the paintings above the doors depicting an *Allegory of the Duc d'Anjou Recognised as the King of Spain* (November 1700) on the right, adjacent to the Apollo Drawing-Room, and an *Allegory of the Revocation of the Edict of Nantes* (1685) on the left, adjacent to the Mars Drawing-Room.

DUC DE SAINT-SIMON,
MEMOIRS

"At the first glance,
when bowing to the King
of Spain [Philippe V] on arriving,
I was so taken aback that
I needed to regain my senses
in order to recover from
the shock. I found no traces
of the Duc d'Anjou
in his countenance,
which had grown considerably
longer and changed,
and which said much less
once he had left France."

Right:
Portrait of
Maria Leczinska,
by Louis Tocqué,
opposite the portrait of
Louis XV,
by Hyacinthe Rigaud

The ceiling painted by Jean-Baptiste de Champaigne shows *Mercury in His Chariot Drawn by Two Cocks*. The ceiling-coves are decorated with four paintings: on the left, adjacent to the Mars Drawing-Room: *Alexander Playing Host to an Embassy of Indians;* at the far end of the room, facing the windows: *Ptolemy Conversing with Scholars in His Library*; and on the right, adjacent to the windows: *Alexander Presenting Aristotle with Various Strange Animals in Order to Write Their History.*

COMTE D'HÉZECQUES, RECOLLECTIONS OF A PAGE IN LOUIS XVI'S COURT

"In the Mercury Drawing-Room stood a clock, once very famous, but less so today as such rapid progress has been made in mechanics. On the hour, cocks would crow and flap their wings. Louis XIV would come out of a temple, and Fame, on a cloud, would crown the Monarch as the bell chimed."

Automaton clock by Antoine Morand

Mercury in His Chariot Drawn by Two Cocks, by Jean-Baptiste de Champaigne

THE APOLLO DRAWING-ROOM

The most sumptuous of all the drawing-rooms of the State Apartment since this was the Throne Room, the Apollo Drawing-Room has retained none of its rich décor. The wall hangings which, in all royal dwellings, varied according to the seasons, were made of crimson velvet trimmed with eighteen strips of gold and silver embroidery in winter, and gold and silver embroidered silk in summer. The silver throne was two metres and sixty centimetres high. When Louis XIV had the silver furniture melted down in 1689, it was replaced by a gilt wood throne the style of which would change with the monarchs. The throne was placed on a dais covered with a Persian carpet with a gold background beneath a canopy, and the three hooks which held it to the wall are still visible. *Apollo in His Chariot Drawn by Four Horses and Accompanied by the Seasons* was painted on the ceiling by Charles de Lafosse (see following page).

The portrait of Louis XIV in his coronation robes, by Hyacinthe Rigaud (right page) is the counterpart of the portrait of Louis XVI, also in his coronation robes, by Antoine-François Callet (below)

COMTE D'HÉZECQUES,
RECOLLECTIONS OF A PAGE
IN LOUIS XVI'S COURT

"In the first drawing-room [...]
named after Apollo,
was a throne of crimson
damask on a dais,
but it was never used.
The King very rarely
held his audiences from atop
the throne, at least not from
that one. In the same room,
a crystal thermometer
was attached to the window,
and the King would come
and check the temperature
several times a day. In addition,
a footman would record
the degrees in his register
three times a day."

THE WAR DRAWING-ROOM

Mansart began building the War Drawing-Room in 1678. Its décor, completed by Le Brun in 1686, celebrates the military victories which led to the Peace of Nijmegen. The walls are lined with marble panels adorned with six gilt-bronze trophies and cascades of weapons. On the wall adjacent to the Apollo Drawing-Room is an oval stucco bas-relief of *Louis XIV on Horseback Riding in Triumph over His Enemies*. This masterpiece by Coysevox is surmounted by two gilt figures representing Fame, and held up by two prisoners in chains. Below, in the bas-relief set into a false fireplace, *Clio Writes the King's History for Posterity*. The ceiling, painted by Le Brun, depicts *France in Arms Seated on a Cloud Surrounded by Victories*. Her shield is decorated with a portrait of Louis XIV. Three conquered enemies are depicted in the ceiling-coves: Germany, on her knees, with an eagle; Spain, threatening, with a roaring lion; and Holland, lying on a lion. The fourth ceiling-cove shows *Bellona, the Goddess of War, Raging with Anger between Rebellion and Discord*.

Prisoner in chains,
by Antoine Coysevox

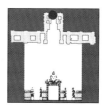

THE HALL OF MIRRORS

The building plans for the Hall of Mirrors, on the site of a terrace built by Le Vau between the apartments of the King and Queen, were presented by J. Hardouin-Mansart and approved in 1678. The Hall of Mirrors which receives light from the seventeen windows overlooking the gardens, reflected in seventeen mirrored arcades, also announced the birth of a French industry: glass production. This nationalist aspect is found in the gilded bronze capitals said to be of the "French Order". This order was created by Le Brun at the request of Colbert so as to establish a new emblem for all national buildings: a fleur-de-lis surmounted by the royal sun on a background of palm leaves and foliage, between two French cocks.

The vault is adorned with thirty compositions by Charles Le Brun and his studio, and is the largest existing pictorial composition in France: it recounts the history of Louis XIV, in the form of ancient allegories, from the start of his personal reign in 1661 until the Peace of Nijmegen in 1678.

The Hall of Mirrors prepared for the signing of the Treaty of Versailles, on 28 June 1919, by Léopold Delbeke

THE HALL OF MIRRORS

The furniture in the State Gallery, as it was then called in the 17th century, was the most sumptuous to say the least: silver tables and great vases for the orange trees, forty-one silver chandeliers and candelabras, white damask curtains embroidered with the royal monogram in gold, and two Savonnerie carpets reflecting the colours of the ceiling. This famous silver furniture was melted down in 1689.

The Hall of Mirrors was essentially used as a passageway, and only served other purposes on exceptional occasions, the most famous of which include the reception of the Ambassadors of Siam in 1686, the Persian Ambassadors in 1715, the marriage of the Duc de Bourgogne to Marie-Adélaïde de Savoie in December 1697, and the masked ball for the wedding of Marie-Antoinette and the Dauphin, the future Louis XVI, in May 1770… This was also where the Treaty of Versailles was signed on 28 June 1919, marking the end of the First World War. Since then, the presidents of the French Republic have continued to hold receptions here for France's official visitors.

The King Rules Alone, 1661, central ceiling composition, by Charles Le Brun

Louis XIV Receiving the Extraordinary Ambassador of Persia in the Hall of Mirrors, on 19 February 1715, by Antoine Coypel. This was the last reception in the reign of Louis XIV, who died on 1 September 1715

State audience granted by Louis XIV for the Doge of Genoa, on 15 May 1685, by Claude Hallé. One can see the silver furniture and throne in particular

MERCURE DE FRANCE, ACCOUNT OF THE RECEPTION OF THE DOGE OF GENOA, ON 15 MAY 1685

"Two things stood out: one was that this apartment and this hall were beautifully furnished, with several millions worth of silver wares; the other was the tremendous crowd everywhere, although these apartments and this hall together could contain as many people as found in the largest palace. Despite the orders given to clear the way along the hall, the Doge had trouble passing through. Field-Marshal Duc de Duras, Captain of the Palace Bodyguards, who had greeted him at the entrance of the guardroom, accompanied him to His Majesty's throne. It was made of silver, and on two raised platforms. Mgr the Dauphin (the Crown Prince) and Monsieur (the King's brother) were next to the King. His Majesty was surrounded by all the Royal Princes, and by his chief officers who held special positions near him during such ceremonies. The Doge's entourage was quite large, most of them being unable to follow him up to the throne, and they took up the empty space in the middle of the hall, which had been cleared to make way for him."

THE PEACE DRAWING-ROOM

In 1712, this drawing-room was separated from the Hall of Mirrors and the War Drawing-Room and annexed to the Queen's Apartment. The connecting archway was closed off by a moving partition and door. This was where the Queen would hold court and also her public games. Here, every Sunday, Maria Leczinska gave concerts of sacred or secular music. It also served as Marie-Antoinette's games room; it was she who installed the gilded bronze "lion" hearth moulded from a model by Boizot.

The ceiling, the work of Le Brun, shows *The Victorious France Offering an Olive Branch to the Powers United against Her. Spain, Christian Europe at Peace, Germany and Holland* are depicted in the ceiling-coves.

Above the fireplace is a large oval painting by François Lemoine in 1729, portraying *Louis XV Bestowing Peace on Europe.*

FÉLIBIEN, ACCOUNT
OF THE FESTIVITIES HELD
AT VERSAILLES ON 18 JULY 1668

"Having granted peace
at the request of his allies
and of all Europe, and shown
signs of unparalleled moderation
and justice, even in the greatest
of his conquests, the King
was now only interested
in ruling his kingdom when,
to compensate for what the Court
had missed during carnival
in his absence, he decided
to organise a gala in the gardens
of Versailles where, in spite
of the pleasures offered
by such a delightful setting,
the mind nonetheless marvelled
at the surprising, extraordinary
beauty with which this great
prince so deftly spices
all his festivities."

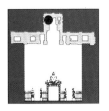

THE QUEEN'S APARTMENT

The Queen's Apartment, overlooking the South Parterre, is symmetrical to the King's State Apartment. Its décor was altered several times during the 18th century. It is now visited in the opposite direction, from the Bedchamber to the Guardroom from which the courtiers entered during the *Ancien Régime*.

Marie-Antoinette playing the harp in her bedchamber at Versailles, by Gautier-Dagoty

THE QUEEN'S BEDCHAMBER

Unlike the King, the Queen only had this one bedchamber. Not only did she sleep here - it was here that the King would join her on certain evenings - but she would also grant her private audiences here in the morning after her toilette. Nineteen "Children of France" were born in this room. Queen Maria-Theresa occupied this bedchamber for a short time from 1682, when the court was finally established at Versailles, until her death on 30 July 1683. She was succeeded by the Dauphines Marie-Christine de Bavière and Marie-Adélaïde de Savoie, followed by the two queens Maria Leczinska (from 1725 to 1768) and Marie-Antoinette (from 1770, when she was still the Dauphine, until 6 October 1789).

THE QUEEN'S BEDCHAMBER

Louis XVI, antique replica by Joseph-Siffrein Duplessis

It was in this room that Marie-Antoinette spent her last night at Versailles. As the rioters made their way to the bedchamber, she was able to escape through one of the two doors behind the wall-hangings at the far end of the alcove leading to the Queen's Private Cabinets. The walls are hung with the "summer furnishings", as they were on the night of the 6th October 1789, when the royal family and the court was forced to leave Versailles for good. The bed and balustrade are modern replicas based on old documents. To the left of the bed is the mahogany, mother-of-pearl and gilded bronze jewellery cabinet made by Ferdinand Schwerdfeger (1787). Above the three mirrors are portraits of the family of Marie-Antoinette: her mother, Maria Theresa, her brother, Joseph II, and her husband, Louis XVI.

DUC DE LUYNES, MEMOIRS OF THE COURT OF LOUIS XV

"Yesterday morning began the re-upholstering of the Queen's bedchamber; complete summer suite with bed, tapestries, armchairs, folding screens, and door curtains.
There are only two armchairs; no more are placed in the Queen's bedchamber. The fabric is from Tours, white, embroidered and painted. The bed and curtains are beautiful and pleasing to the eye. In the centre of each tapestry panel is a large vase, which is striking; but the ornaments that go with it are all off-centre as is the new fashion."

Maria Theresa of Austria, mother of Marie-Antoinette, tapestry executed at the Gobelins works by Michel-Henri Cozette after a portrait by Joseph Ducreux

Joseph II, brother of Marie-Antoinette, tapestry executed at the Gobelins works by Michel-Henri Cozette after a portrait by Joseph Ducreux

THE SALON DES NOBLES

It was in this room, equivalent to the throne room (Apollo Drawing-Room) in the King's State Apartment, that the Queen held her official audiences, and ladies newly admitted to Court were presented to her. The Queen's throne, placed on a platform at the far end of the room, was covered with a canopy, the hooks of which are still visible. All that remains of the original décor is the ceiling painted by Michel Corneille, depicting *Mercury Spreading His Influence over the Arts and Sciences*.

In 1785, when Marie-Antoinette had the room re-decorated, the walls were lined with apple-green damask, and Jean-Baptiste Regnault executed the two paintings situated above the doors: *The Origin of Painting* and *Pygmalion Praying to Venus to Bring His Statue to Life*. Two chests of drawers (the third has not been found) and the two corner cupboards by Riesener decorated with bronzes embossed by Gouthière, similar to those on the new slate-blue marble fireplace, were also installed at that time.

The portrait of Louis XV in royal dress, a tapestry executed by Cozette after the painting by L.-M. van Loo, hangs in the same place as in the time of Marie-Antoinette.

Head of Mercury in gilded stucco in the ceiling frame

*Madame Elisabeth,
Aunt of Louis XVI,
by Adélaïde
Labille-Guiard*

*Right page:
Marie-Antoinette
and Her Children
(Madame Royale,
the first Dauphin
who died in 1789,
and the Duc de
Normandie, the
future Louis XVII),
by Elisabeth
Vigée-Lebrun*

THE ANTECHAMBER OF THE GRAND COUVERT

Visitors who had obtained an audience with the Queen would wait here before being received. The name *"Grand Couvert"* stems from the fact that in the 18th century the sovereigns would eat their public meals in this room. The Marquise de la Tour du Pin, daughter-in-law of the Minister of War, gave an account of one such ceremonial meal which she attended in 1788: "The Queen sat to the left of the King. They had their backs to the fireplace, and a row of stools, on which were seated the duchesses, princesses, or senior officers having the privilege of a stool, was arranged in a circle facing them. Behind these stood the other ladies, facing the King and Queen. The King ate with a hearty appetite, but the Queen did not remove her gloves or use her serviette, which was not at all proper."

On certain evenings, Marie-Antoinette gave balls and the appearance of the room would be completely transformed.

THE GUARDROOM

In the same way as its symmetrical counterpart, the Diana Drawing-Room in the King's State Apartment, was reached by the Ambassadors' Staircase, this Guardroom communicates with the Queen's Staircase. It provides access to the former common guardroom of the King's and Queen's guards, now the *Salle du Sacre* or Coronation Room. To the right of the fireplace, a staircase leads to the Dauphin's and Dauphine's Apartments, the Mesdames Apartments, and the Queen's Private Rooms on the ground floor.

Noël Coypel painted the ceiling compositions for the former Jupiter Drawing-Room, which became the War Drawing-Room in 1678. The five compositions: *Jupiter Accompanied by Justice* (in the centre), *Ptolemy Philadelphus Freeing the Jews, Alexander Severus Distributing Wheat to the People during the Famine, Trajan Dispensing Justice* and *Solon Explaining His Laws* (in the ceiling-coves) were installed in this room in 1680.

COMTE D'HÉZECQUES, RECOLLECTIONS OF A PAGE IN LOUIS XVI'S COURT

"In the château, the bodyguards' duty was to stand guard at the doors of the apartments, man their weapons when the princes passed, fill up the chapel during Mass and escort the Royal Family to dinner. They had to be able to recognise dukes and other peers, because the sentinel had to present arms and click his right heel twice when these persons passed. In addition, this sentinel had to open the door and keep it from being opened; but this guard seemed to be rather easy going, and was excluded from all of these functions."

Sacrifice to Jupiter, by Noël Coypel

ORDERS

FOR THE QUEEN'S SENTINEL

The sentinel of the Queen's room will not allow any unknown priests or friars to pass without the Captain's permission; even with the Captain's permission, he will not allow them to enter the Grand Couvert unless under special orders.

He will not allow any unknown person, anyone who looks unwell or any person recently afflicted by smallpox to pass.

No sedan chairs other than those of the Royal Family, or princes and princesses of royal blood are to remain in the room.

The presence of liverymen is not permitted.

The livery of the princes and princesses of royal blood, the Chevalier of the Legion of Honour, ladies-in-waiting and mistresses of the robes, and the chief chaplain to the Queen will go through into the antechamber.

He will allow only one servant of the cardinals and ministers to pass.

THE SALLE DU SACRE

Originally the common guardroom of the King's and Queen's guards, this room is named after the replica painted by David himself, between 1808 and 1822, of the famous painting depicting the coronation of Napoleon I and Josephine on 2 December 1804, now in the Louvre. The other paintings all relate to the Napoleonic era. They were exhibited here on the orders of Louis-Philippe when, in 1837, he transformed Versailles into a Museum of French History. Two large compositions, one by David: *The Distribution of Eagle Standards on the Champs-de-Mars* (1804), and the other by Gros: *The Battle of Aboukir* (1799), cover the eastern and northern walls. The paintings above the doors, by Gérard, depict *Courage, Genius, Generosity and Constance*, and *The Allegory of the 18th Brumaire* on the ceiling is the work of Callet. In the centre of room stands a bronze and porcelain column commissioned by Napoleon I to commemorate the Battle of Austerlitz (2 December 1805).

The coronation of Napoleon I and Josephine, on 2 December 1804, by Jacques-Louis David

COMTE D'HÉZECQUES, RECOLLECTIONS
OF A PAGE IN LOUIS XVI'S COURT

"On the morning of Maundy Thursday, twelve young children were lined up in the main Guardroom, their freshness equal to that of the enormous bouquet of the rarest flowers they held in their hands. [...]

The ceremony began at nine o'clock with a sermon. On that day, the preacher could voice all the vehemence of his zeal and thunder loudly against the abuses and scandals of the court. [...]

Each child held his right foot over a vermeil basin held by a chaplain; the Comte d'Artois poured a few drops of water over it; Monsieur wiped it with the towel the child wore around his neck, and the King kissed the foot."

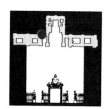

THE HALL
OF BATTLES

The South Wing, also known as the Princes' Wing, once consisted of five large apartments on the first floor, for the members of the royal family, and fourteen apartments in the attic storey, which could be subdivided, for the courtiers.

The Hall of Battles desired by Louis-Philippe forced the architects, Fontaine and Nepveu, to demolish these apartments dating from the *Ancien Régime*. The Hall, 120 metres long and 13 metres wide, contains thirty-five large paintings portraying fourteen centuries of French history through its great military victories, from Tolbiac, won by Clovis in 496, to Wagram, a victory for Napoleon I in 1809. The eighty-two busts represent some of the most famous French soldiers who died in combat.

Saint Louis at the Battle of Taillebourg, on 21 July 1242 (detail), by Eugène Delacroix

TOUR OF THE KING'S BEDCHAMBER

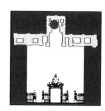

THE KING'S APARTMENT

When the court was finally established at Versailles, the State Apartment became a ceremonial apartment, and it was here that the life of Louis XIV, every moment of which being dictated by etiquette, effectively unfolded. In its present state, the King's Apartment consists of five rooms: a guardroom, a first antechamber where the King dined in public at the *"Grand Couvert"*, a second antechamber, known as the Antechamber of the *Œil-de-Bœuf* or bullseye, and a bedchamber which was only installed here in 1701. The King's Apartment corresponds to Louis XIV's perception of his role as monarch: he was duty bound to be "visible" at all times. His successors would arrange the space in a manner more favourable to their private existence, but until the end of the *Ancien Régime*, the King's Apartment would remain a place in which his power would be represented.

THE MARBLE STAIRCASE

This much frequented staircase led to the King's Apartment, and also to the Queen's Apartment and the apartment of Madame de Maintenon whom Louis XIV secretly married after the death of Queen Maria-Theresa. Lavishly decorated with marble, like all of the State Apartments, the Marble Staircase was built in 1681 when it became the counterpart to the Ambassadors' Staircase which, on the other side of the courtyard, led to the King's State Apartment.

The Young Louis XIV, attributed to Charles Le Brun

THE ANTECHAMBER
OF THE ŒIL-DE-BŒUF

This second antechamber only dates from 1701. It previously consisted of two rooms, one of which had originally served as the King's Bedchamber for seventeen years. The Antechamber of the *Œil-de-Bœuf* is named after the oval window in the cornice decorated with a ring of children, the style and charm of which are reminiscent of 18th-century art.

COMTE D'HÉZECQUES,
RECOLLECTIONS OF A PAGE
IN LOUIS XVI'S COURT

"At the hour of the levee,
a crowd of courtiers from Versailles
or Paris would assemble
at the château… Everyone would
wait in the antechamber or
the hall for the moment when
the King would rise,
and those called by their service
or who had an entrance
into the bedchamber,
would wait in the *Œil-de-Bœuf*…"

THE KING'S BEDCHAMBER

It was only in 1701 that the King's Bedchamber was installed here at the centre of the château, when Louis XIV was aged 63. This was the setting for the ceremonies of the *Lever* and the *Coucher*, and also a large part of the daily life of the King, who took his lunch here at the *"Petit Couvert"*, and also granted audiences in this room.

During the *Lever*, which lasted almost an hour, there were six successive entrances which marked the rank of each courtier. The King was washed, brushed and dressed in front of a crowd of several hundred people. The room has retained its original décor and certain paintings, namely: *The Four Evangelists* and *Caesar's Denarius*, by Valentin de Boulogne, *Saint John the Baptist*, by Carraciolo, *Mary Magdalene* by Domenichino, and the *Self-portrait* and *Portrait of the Marquis de Moncade*, by van Dyck.

First Nomination of the Knights of the Order of Saint Louis, Taking Place in the King's Bedchamber, by François Marot

Keeper of the Sleeve in the reign of Louis XV

THE COUNCIL CHAMBER

During the reign of Louis XIV, this was the site of two chambers, in one of which the King would hold his Councils every day at the end of the morning. In 1755, Louis XV made it into one room with wooden panelling designed by Gabriel and carved by Antoine Rousseau. Two antique busts of *Alexander the Great* and *Scipio Africanus* were also placed in this room. For more than a century, all important political decisions were made in this room, including in 1775 the decision to participate in the War of Independence which would lay the foundations of the United States of America.

SAINT SIMON, MEMOIRS
"The Council of State
was held on Sunday,
and often on Mondays;
Tuesdays, Council of Finances;
Wednesdays, Council of State;
Saturdays, Council
of finances [...]
Thursday mornings were
almost always free. It was also
a big day for the bastards,
the Builders, and the house
valets, because the King
had nothing to do. Friday after
Mass was confession time,
and since there were no other
appointments, this could last
until dinner time [...]"

*Alexander the Great,
antique bust restored
in the 17ᵗʰ century*

*Fireplace
detail*

THE DAUPHIN'S AND DAUPHINE'S APARTMENTS

These apartments underwent numerous alterations and had several occupants, all of which were close relations of the King. They have been recreated according to their appearance in the 18th century, or more precisely between 1747 and 1765, when they were occupied by Louis, Dauphin of France, son of Louis XV, and his second wife Maria-Josepha of Saxony.

Left page:
The Dauphine's
Private Cabinet

Left:
The Dauphin's
Library

*A farm, by Queen
Maria Leczinska,
in the style of
Jean-Baptiste Oudry*

PRINCESS PALATINE,
MARLY, 18 FEBRUARY 1712

"I thought I had finished
telling you sad news,
with the exception
of the painful ceremony
I attended yesterday
at Versailles; but disaster
has struck once again.
Our good Crown Prince has
followed his wife to the grave,
he died at eight thirty.
I'm sure you can imagine how
disconsolate we all are here.
The King's pain is so great
that I fear for his health. [...]
As the King has an awful cold,
he was not wakened,
but was given the terrible news
when he awoke."

THE DAUPHIN'S BEDCHAMBER

The occupants of this room, prior to the Dauphin, the son of Louis XV, included Monseigneur, the son of Louis XIV, who exhibited his collection of objets d'art in this room. It was also the room of the Regent Philippe d'Orléans who died in this apartment on 2 December 1723. The present size of the bedchamber corresponds to its appearance in 1747 when the wooden panelling carved by Verberckt to Gabriel's designs and the griotte marble fireplace decorated with bronze figures of Flora and Zephyr, by Jacques Caffieri, were installed. The "duchess" style bed was executed in approximately 1740 for the Marquise de Créquy. To the right of the bed hangs a picture of a farm painted by Queen Maria Leczinska under the supervision of her drawing master Jean-Baptiste Oudry.

THE DAUPHINE'S STATE CHAMBER

The tour of the Dauphine's Apartment follows on from the Dauphin's Apartment, but in the opposite sequence. In the 18th century, one would enter via the first antechamber, which led to the second antechamber, the State Chamber, the Bedchamber and, lastly, the Private Cabinet. The ladies in the Dauphine's circle would meet in this large room to converse or to play. A series of portraits of royal figures or ministers from the start of Louis XV's reign are now displayed in this room. The only original part of the décor is the console table on which stands the barometer commissioned for the future Louis XVI. He occupied this apartment until 1774, the date of his accession to the throne.

Queen Maria Leczinska and the Dauphin, by Alexis-Simon Belle, 1729

THE DAUPHINE'S BEDCHAMBER

The compositions above the doors: *Psyche Fleeing the Wrath of Venus* and *Psyche Begging Venus for Forgiveness*, painted by Jean Restout, are part of the décor dating from 1747. The "Polish" style bed (of excellent quality) was made by Nicolas Heurtaut, but is not that belonging to the Dauphine Maria-Josepha of Saxony, who gave birth to three future kings in this room: Louis XVI, Louis XVIII and Charles X. The paintings hanging on either side of the bed are two portraits of the daughters of Louis XV, by Jean-Marc Nattier: *Madame Henriette as Flora* and *Madame Adélaïde as Diana*. The oval painting to the left of the bed represents *Madame Louise and Madame Henriette* by Pierre Gobert.

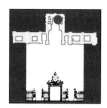

THE KING'S PRIVATE APARTMENT

During the reign of Louis XIV, this was a series of cabinets which contained some of the King's collections, including the famous *Mona Lisa*, and where only a few guests of honour, scholars and artists were admitted on rare occasions. Work was begun in 1735 to create a proper apartment for Louis XV, with a guardroom on the ground floor, a first antechamber *(Cabinet des Chiens)*, a second antechamber (the Clock Cabinet), a study (Private Cabinet), and a bedchamber.

LOUIS XV'S BEDCHAMBER

From 1722, when Louis XV returned to Versailles, and until 1738, the young king slept in the bedchamber of his great-grandfather. However, it was so uncomfortable that he decided to alter this bedchamber to make it smaller and more appropriately situated. The ceremonies of the *Lever* and the *Coucher* continued to take place in the "Bedchamber of Louis XIV", a tradition that would be continued by Louis XVI. The alcove, where the bed was once situated, is hung with a gold embroidered lampas fabric, recreating the wall-hangings found there in 1789.

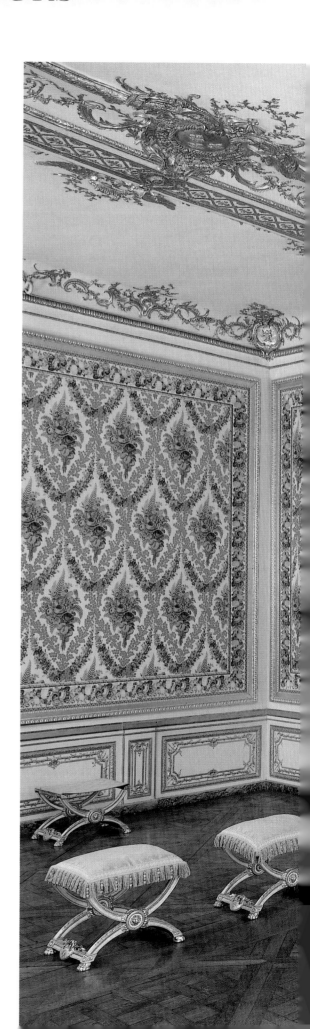

THE CLOCK CABINET

This cabinet was named after the extraordinary astronomical clock by Passemant which was installed in 1754. The barometer by Lemaire and Mazière, commissioned by Louis XV but only installed in 1827, stands opposite. On the floor, a copper line represents the meridian of Paris.

The clock indicates the time, the day, the month, the year, and the phase of the moon. Inside the crystal globe, one can see the planets revolving around the sun

THE PRIVATE CABINET

Formerly Louis XIV's picture gallery, the Private Cabinets opened onto the adjoining rooms through the arcades (Clock Cabinet and *Cabinet des Dépêches*), which Louis XV had closed in 1738. At that time, he commissioned Gaudreaux, the cabinet-maker, to fashion the medal cabinet in the form of a chest of drawers. The other major alterations were made in 1753, when the walls were lined with wainscoting designed by Gabriel and carved by Verbeckt. However, the main feature of this room is still the roll-top writing desk commissioned in 1760 from Oeben, who died before it was finished. It was only completed by Riesener nine years later. The mechanism makes it possible to release or fix at the same time, by a quarter turn of the key, both the leaf of the desk and all of the drawers, with the exception of two drawers situated on the sides which enabled the King's servants to refill the ink pots.

THE BATHROOM

Decorated between 1770 and 1773, this was the seventh and last bathroom installed for Louis XV at Versailles. The window then opened onto a courtyard known as "the courtyard of the King's cellar", which was later replaced by a staircase built in the 19th century, during the reign of Louis-Philippe. Only the wooden panelling carved by Antoine Rousseau and his sons, depicting the pleasures of water, serves as a reminder that this was once a bathroom. However, it was not used as such by Louis XVI who installed his "Privy Purse Cabinet" here, where he kept his private account ledgers up to date.

This chest of drawers, which had originally been commissioned for Fontainebleau in 1778, was brought on the orders of Louis XVI to his library at Versailles, and has recently returned to this room.

LOUIS XVI'S LIBRARY

After the death of his grandfather in 1774, Louis XVI, while at Compiègne, sent orders to the architect Gabriel to implement the plans, which had already been drafted, to create this library. This was previously the bedchamber of Madame Adélaïde for whom Louis XV had installed an apartment consisting of 5 rooms, a suite which he annexed to his own Private Apartment in 1769. The table was made for this room by Riesener. The table top is made from a single piece of mahogany measuring 2.10 metres in diameter.

THE PORCELAIN DINING ROOM

In 1769, Louis XV created this dining-room where, until 1789, the King took his non-official suppers - to which forty or so people would be invited. During the reign of Louis XVI, the latest pieces produced by the Sèvres Porcelain Factory were exhibited here every year at Christmas.

The Sèvres porcelain plaques were commissioned by Louis XVI in the style of the tapestries depicting *The Hunts of Louis XV,* by Jean-Baptiste Oudry.

Above: Stag staying close to the hounds in the Franchard rocks in the forest of Fontainebleau

Left: The small quarry given to the young hounds, "Fohu à la fin de la curée"

LOUIS XVI'S GAMES ROOM

There are no traces of Louis XIV's Cabinet of Curios and Rare Objects which so dazzled visitors with its lavish collections. In 1753, this room became an antechamber to Madame Adélaïde's apartment, which Louis XV had rearranged in 1769. However, it was his grandson who transformed it into a games room. A large part of the furniture dispersed during the Revolution has been found and returned to its original place: the four corner cupboards commissioned from Riesener in 1774, and the chairs designed by Boulard in 1785.

The gouaches by van Blarenberghe, chosen by Louis XVI, commemorate the military victories of his grandfather.

MEMOIRS OF M. DE SÉGURET, CHIEF CLERK OF LOUIS XVI'S PRIVATE APARTMENTS

"I can attest that His Majesty often took his coffee much colder then you or I [...] During that time, the guests would be crammed into the drawing-room. Monsieur arranged a game of whist, and Monsieur le Comte d'Artois played billiards. When the King finally came back into the drawing-room, he arranged a game of backgammon at one ecu per piece. He did not like to play for high stakes, and one ecu was his limit."

Backgammon table for Louis XVI's Games Room

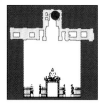

THE KING'S PRIVATE CABINETS

On four levels, around the Courtyard of the Stags and in the attics overlooking the courtyards at the entrance to the château, Louis XV created a private area, inaccessible to courtiers. This consisted of a maze of rooms: dining-rooms, kitchens, laboratories, bathrooms, libraries and workshops, and it was also in these private cabinets that Madame Du Barry, the last mistress of Louis XV, lived after the death of his wife. After the death of Louis XV, Madame Du Barry was banished and her apartment given to Thierry de Ville d'Avray, the King's first valet, and the Duc de Villequier, the chief lord-in-waiting. However, Louis XVI continued to use the other cabinets, and since his liking for the technical arts was known, it was not surprising to find a carpentry cabinet, a woodwork lathe cabinet, a legendary iron-work studio, and a room with a lathe for mechanics...

The King's Staircase leading to the King's Private Cabinets

Right page: Suite of rooms in Madame Du Barry's apartment

MARIE-ANTOINETTE'S PRIVATE ROOMS

THE GILDED CABINET

Queen Maria-Theresa, wife of Louis XIV, who died shortly after the Court was finally established at Versailles, had only an oratory and a boudoir for her private rooms. It was at the time of Maria Leczinska that these rooms situated behind the Queen's Bedchamber began to multiply. However, their greatest extension was during the occupancy of Marie-Antoinette.

The Queen's Private Cabinet, known as the Gilded Cabinet, is the largest of the Queen's private rooms. It was here that Marie-Antoinette would receive her friends, and also her favourite painter Madame Vigée-Lebrun, her appointed milliner, Rose Bertin, and her music teacher, Grétry. Redecorated in 1783, in the "antique" style in fashion at the end of the 18th century, the room now contains numerous pieces of furniture which once belonged to Marie-Antoinette: the chest of drawers by Riesener came from her bedchamber at the Château de Marly, and the seats and chandelier from her apartment at the Château de Saint-Cloud. The door to the left of the fireplace opens into a small cabinet adorned with wooden panelling painted in *vernis Martin*.

THE MERIDIAN CABINET

The décor of this room was commissioned by Louis XVI in 1781 on the birth of the Dauphin, and consisted of numerous symbols relating to the event itself and conjugal love. Marie-Antoinette used to come here to rest at midday, hence the name "Meridian". This small octagonal room allowed her to withdraw from her state apartment and escape the constraints of etiquette.

THE LIBRARY

The library, which achieved its present form in 1781, had an annex (below) built onto it in 1783, destined to house large works. This collection was destroyed during the Revolution, but a few books embossed with the royal arms of Marie-Antoinette or her family have been replaced.

THE BILLIARDS CABINET

The Queen had other cabinets on the second floor. One of these, the silk hangings of which have just been restored and the settees by J. Jacob replaced, was the billiards cabinet.

MESDAMES VICTOIRE'S AND ADÉLAÏDE'S APARTMENTS

Part of these apartments (Madame Victoire's apartments) corresponds to what was one of the most beautiful places in the château: Louis XIV's Bath Apartment. The walls and floor were lined with inlaid polychrome marble, and at the centre of the bathroom was an octagonal pool which has been preserved and is now located in the Orangery. The two elder daughters of Louis XV, Madame Adélaïde (1732-1800) and Madame Victoire (1733-1799) lived in these apartments until the Revolution which forced them into exile.

"Madame Adélaïde was the eldest of the five princesses. She did not wish to marry, preferring her status as a Daughter of France.
She held Court until the death of Louis XV. One of her sisters, Madame Infante, reigned rather sadly in Parma; another, Madame Louise, was a Carmelite nun. Of the five princesses, she seemed the most refined, without comparison.
She passionately enjoyed every pleasure, appreciated good food, was extremely concerned with her appearance, had an extreme yearning for luxurious pursuits, a rather lively imagination and, lastly, a great tendency towards coquetry.
Thus, when the King entered Madame Adélaïde's bedchamber to tell her that Madame Louise had left in the night, her first cry was "With whom?""

The numerous paintings on display, in addition to their artistic quality, also provide an excellent account of life at Court in the 18th century: the portrait of Madame Adélaïde (left page) by Jean-Marc Nattier gives an idea of the sumptuous court dress, whereas *The Family of the Duc de Penthièvre*, known as *The Cup of Chocolate*, portrays an intimate scene from the life of a princely family.

The Family of the Duc de Penthièvre, known as The Cup of Chocolate, by Jean-Baptiste Charpentier, 1768

THE OPERA

The Opera experienced a long gestation period since there was a gap of more than eighty years between the first plans dating from the reign of Louis XIV and the creation of the opera-house in 1770. An event as important as the marriage of the Dauphin, the future Louis XVI, to the Archduchess of Austria, Marie-Antoinette, was required in order to finally release the necessary funds. The architect Gabriel, who had been working on the project since 1748, had only twenty-three months in order to complete the project. The opera-house was entirely built of wood for reasons of both economy and acoustics. The engineer Arnoult designed a mechanism which would raise the stalls to the same level as the stage, one of the largest in France, so that balls and prestigious receptions could be held there in addition to operas and concerts. Below, the machinery occupied an area the height of which reached "approximately half the height of the towers of Notre-Dame", according to the Duc de Croÿ in his *Journal* on 16 May 1770. The decorative sculpture is the work of Augustin Pajou's studio.

The banquet held here on 1 October 1789, for the officers of the Kings' Bodyguard, caused a great stir. This event was not unrelated to the fact that on 6 October the Parisians invaded the château and forced the royal family to leave Versailles for good. The opera was not used again until 1837, when the museum created by Louis-Philippe was inaugurated. In 1871, it was the seat of the French National Assembly, followed by the Senate from 1876 to 1879.

Bas-relief by Augustin Pajou

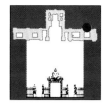

THE REVOLUTION ROOMS

These rooms return to the context of Louis-Philippe's Museum of French History. Four rooms depict a few moments of the 1789 French Revolution. The beginnings are portrayed by the large sketch of *The Jeu de Paume Oath of Allegiance* (20 June 1789) by David. A painting by Hubert Robert illustrates *The Celebrations in Honour of the Federation at Champs-de-Mars, 14 July 1790*, and that by Jacques Berteaux represents the storming of the Tuileries on 10 August 1792, when the Monarchy collapsed. The portrait of Marie-Antoinette painted by Kucharski in 1792 received two pike blows which are still visible.

Above:
The Jeu de Paume Oath of Allegiance at Versailles on 20 June 1789, by Jacques-Louis David

Left:
The Jeu de Paume Oath of Allegiance, painted sketch by Jacques-Louis David

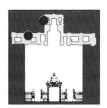

THE CONSULATE
AND EMPIRE ROOMS

Situated on the second floor, in the Chimay attic storey (above the Queen's Apartment) and in the attics and ground floor of the South Wing, are 31 rooms dedicated to the man once known as General Bonaparte and who became Emperor on 2 December 1804, under the name of Napoleon I.

Versailles has a vast collection of paintings depicting the Napoleonic era and the Imperial family since Louis-Philippe gathered almost all the paintings commissioned by Napoleon I to extol his own glory. In 1837, the museum "dedicated to the glories of France" could not ignore the Emperor who, despite being dead for over fifteen years, still had numerous partisans.

Napoleon Bonaparte,
First Consul Standing
Before a View of Anvers,
by Jean-Baptiste Greuze

Napoleon Holding Forth
to the 2nd Corps
of the Grande Armée
Before the Attack on Augsbourg,
by Claude Gautherot

Right page:
The General Bonaparte
on the Bridge of Arcole,
17 November 1796,
by Antoine-Jean Gros

THE 19TH CENTURY ROOMS

In addition to the Restoration (from 1814 to 1830) and the July Monarchy (from 1830 to 1848), these rooms are also dedicated to the Second Empire (from 1852 to 1870), and the Third Republic up to the First World War. After the fall of its founder in 1848, the Museum of French History went on to expand its collections.

It illustrates not only the most significant historical events, but also the political figures and artists who marked the century: Lamartine, Baudelaire, Stendhal, Hugo, Mallarmé, and Debussy…

Louis-Philippe I, King of the French (1773-1850), and the 1830 Charter, in the style of Winterhalter

Right page:
Entry of Charles X into Paris on 6 June 1825, by Louis-François Lejeune

WALKS IN THE GARDENS

TO THE WEST

Work to replant the gardens has been under way since 1992, but due to the devastating storm of December 1999, it will take several decades for the gardens to regain their appearance.

The Grand Perspective opens up before the onlooker observing the gardens from the Hall of Mirrors, drawing the eye from the Water Parterre towards the horizon. Le Nôtre took pleasure in developing and extending the original perspective, existing before the reign of Louis XIV, by widening the Royal Avenue and digging the Grand Canal.

THE WATER PARTERRE

The two ponds of the Water Parterre appear as a continuation of the château façade. Often modified, their definitive appearance was only achieved in 1685. The sculptural décor was inspired and supervised by Charles Le Brun: each pond is adorned with four recumbent statues depicting the rivers and streams of France, together with four nymphs and four groups of children. From 1687 to 1694, the models designed by the sculptors (Tuby, Le Hongre, Regnaudin, and Coysevox etc.) were cast in bronze by the Keller brothers, metal-founders, at the Paris Arsenal.

The Marne,
by Le Hongre

Below:
The Rhône, by Tuby

COLBERT, ORDERS
AND REGULATIONS
FOR THE BUILDINGS
OF VERSAILLES,
24 OCTOBER 1674

"Inspect every pump twice a week.
Make sure that nothing
is missing and always have
a second set of shafts, boards
and bolts for all the devices…
Constantly inspect
all the fountains and count
the number of workmen Denis
[the head fountain master]
has according to his contract."

The Garonne, by Coysevox,

Fighting animals, bloodhound killing a stag, by Houzeau

The Water Parterre is not complete without the two fountains, known as the Fighting Animals, completed in 1687, which flank the stairway leading to the Fountain of Latona, or the six allegorical statues: Air (by Le Hongre), Evening (by Desjardins), Noon and Daybreak (by G. Marsy), Spring (by Magnier), and Water (by Le Gros), which were part of Colbert's "Great Commission" of marble statues in 1674.

THE FOUNTAIN OF LATONA

Inspired by Ovid's *Metamorphosis*, the Fountain of Latona illustrates the legend of the mother of Apollo and Diana protecting her children from the insults of the Lycian peasants, and imploring Jupiter to avenge her. The central marble group depicting Latona and her children, carved by the Marsy brothers, originally stood on a rock in 1670. This was surrounded by six frogs half-emerging from the water, and twenty-four other frogs arranged outside the fountain on a grassy platform. The goddess then faced the château.

The fountain was modified by Jules Hardouin-Mansart between 1687 and 1689. The rock was replaced by concentric marble bases, and the Latona group now looks towards the Grand Canal. The Fountain of Latona is extended by a parterre on which the two Lizard Fountains are situated.

THE LATONA PARTERRE

Eighteen statues (nine on each side) border the Latona inclines, including *Lyrical Poem*, by Tuby, Fire, by Dossier, and *Melancholy*, by La Perdrix which were part of the "Great Commission" of 1674, when Colbert commissioned work from numerous sculptors as part of the iconographical programme devised by Charles Le Brun. The crescent around the Latona Parterre, which leads to the Royal Avenue, is interspersed with ten statues including four famous groups dating from the reign of Louis XIV: *Castor and Pollux*, by Coysevox, *Aria and Poetus*, by Lespingola, *Peace among the Greeks*, by Carlier and Mosnier, and *Laocoön and his sons*, by Tuby.

COLBERT, ORDERS
AND REGULATIONS
FOR THE BUILDINGS
OF VERSAILLES,
24 OCTOBER 1674
"He shall frequently
inspect all the buildings
along the canal,
and review the number
of men he employs,
and send me a certificate
every month."

THE ROYAL AVENUE

Also known as the *"Tapis Vert"*, due to the wide strip of grass at the centre of the avenue, the Royal Avenue measures 335 metres long and 40 metres wide. The outline dates from the reign of Louis XIII; however, Le Nôtre enlarged and adorned the avenue with twelve statues and twelve vases (arranged in symmetrical pairs). Most of these were works sent by pupils from the French Academy in Rome in the 17th century. Avenues on either side lead to the different groves waiting to be discovered by visitors to the gardens.

THE FOUNTAIN OF APOLLO AND THE GRAND CANAL

From 1636, under Louis XIII, a pond (known as Swan Pond) existed on this site, which Louis XIV had enlarged and adorned with the famous magnificent gilded lead group depicting Apollo in his chariot, executed by Tuby from Le Brun's designs. Tuby worked on this monumental group at the Gobelins works from 1668 to 1670, when it was brought to Versailles, and gilded and installed the following year.

This was followed by construction work on the Grand Canal which lasted eleven years (1668 to 1679). The Grand Canal was the scene of numerous nautical festivities, and many small boats sailed on it. From 1669, Louis XIV commissioned rowing boats and reduced-scale ships. In 1674, the Republic of Venice sent the King two gondolas and four gondoliers, who were housed in a series of buildings at the top of the canal, later known as Little Venice.

Louis XIV,
The Manner of Presenting
the Gardens of Versailles

"Walk down to Apollo,
and pause to contemplate
the figures, the vases along
the Royal Avenue, Latona
and the château;
one can also see the canal.
If one wishes to see
the Menagerie and Trianon
on the same day,
this should be done before
seeing the other fountains."

TO THE NORTH

In the northern part of the gardens, water is the predominant theme, probably because the natural incline of the land enables a multiplicity of water effects. However, the Grotto of Thetis, which already attracted numerous visitors due to its varied water effects and beautiful interior décor, was situated close by until 1684.

The same principle of a central avenue, opening up the view and bordered with tree-lined groves, which characterises the east-west axis, has been applied here. A stairway, the Pyramid Fountain (the counterpart of the Fountain of Latona), the Water Avenue (which opens up the perspective in the same way as the Royal Avenue), and lastly the Dragon Fountain (the theme of which runs parallel with the Fountain of Apollo) lead to a vast expanse of water: the Fountain of Neptune.

The Knife-Grinder,
by Foggini and Chaste Venus,
after Coysevox

THE NORTH PARTERRE

From the central terrace and the Water Parterre, the North Parterre, developed in 1664, is reached by a few steps flanked by two bronze sculptures: *Chaste Venus*, after Coysevox, and the *Knife-Grinder*, by Foggini. The two Crown Ponds are situated on each side of the central avenue, filled with swimming lead tritons and mermaids, the work of Tuby and Le Hongre. The North Parterre is surrounded by eighteen sculptures, fifteen of which date from the Great Commission of 1674. The iconographical programme devised by Charles Le Brun depicts the myth of Apollo and his beneficial and influential course around the earth. The statues are divided into groups of four: the four continents, the four seasons, and the four temperaments… However, the perpetual changes to the layout of the gardens soon caused the group to be dispersed.

THE PYRAMID FOUNTAIN

Executed by Girardon according to a design by Le Brun, the Pyramid Fountain took three years to build. The fountain is made up of four marble bowls placed one on top the other, supported by lead tritons, dolphins and crayfish.

THE BATHING NYMPHS

Running down from the Pyramid Fountain, the cascade, known as the *Nymphs of Diana Bathing*, is adorned with bas-reliefs, the most famous of which on the supporting wall, made of lead and originally gilded, is the work of Girardon (1668-1670). The other bas-reliefs are by Le Gros, Le Hongre and Magnier.

Nymphs of Diana Bathing, by Girardon

THE WATER AVENUE

According to his brother Charles (famous author of tales), it was Claude Perrault (the architect) who originally designed this avenue, also known as the *Allée des Marmousets* (a colloquial word originating from *"marmots"* which literally means "kids" or children). The Water Avenue is flanked by twenty-two groups cast in bronze, crowned with bowls carved from Languedoc marble.

THE DRAGON FOUNTAIN

The Water Avenue leads via a crescent to the Dragon Fountain, which depicts an episode from the legend of Apollo: Python, the serpent (slain by the arrow of the young Apollo), is surrounded by dolphins and cupids armed with bows and arrows, riding on swans. The main water jet reaches a height of twenty-seven metres. On each side of the fountain are avenues leading to two groves currently being restored: to the east is the *Bosquet de la France Triomphante*, and to the west is the *Bosquet des Trois Fontaines*.

THE FOUNTAIN OF NEPTUNE

The Fountain of Neptune, then known as the pond "below the Dragon", or the *"Pièce des Sapins"*, was built between 1679 and 1681, under the supervision of Le Nôtre. Jacques-Ange Gabriel slightly modified the shape of the fountain in 1736, and the sculptural décor was installed in 1740, consisting of three groups: *Neptune and Amphitrite* by L.-S. Adam, *Proteus* by Bouchardon, and *The god Oceanus* by J.-B. Lemoyne. The new fountain, inaugurated by Louis XV, was greatly admired due to the number, range and variety of water jets playing on the lead sculptures. The fountain comprises ninety-nine water effects forming a magnificent hydraulic group.

TO THE SOUTH

THE SOUTH PARTERRE

The best view of the South Parterre is probably from the windows of the Queen's Apartment on the first floor of the château. Formerly known as the "Flower Parterre" or the "Parterre of Love", the South Parterre is situated above the Orangery built by Jules Hardouin-Mansart. It is reached by a few steps flanked by two of the oldest pieces of sculpture in the park: *Children Riding on a Sphinx*. The bronze children were modelled by Sarazin, cast by Duval in 1668, and placed on marble sphinxes carved by Lerambert.

Sleeping Ariadne, classical replica by Van Clève

LOUIS XIV, THE MANNER
OF PRESENTING
THE GARDENS OF VERSAILLES

"Then turn left and pass between
the Sphinxes [...]
at the level of the Sphinxes,
pause to look at the South
Parterre, then go straight
to the top of the Orangery
where one can see
the Orangery Parterre
and the Pond of the Swiss."

THE ORANGERY

Built by Jules Hardouin-Mansart between 1684 and 1686, to replace the small orangery erected by Le Vau in 1663, the Orangery consists of a central arched gallery, 155 metres long, which is extended by two lateral galleries beneath the Hundred Steps. Light enters the whole building through large arched windows. The Orangery Parterre spreads over three hectares; during the reign of Louis XIV, it was adorned with a few sculptures now in the Louvre Museum. The 1055 trees planted in boxes (palm trees, oleanders, pomegranate trees, Eugenia trees and orange trees…) are taken out onto the Orangery Parterre, consisting of four grassy areas and a circular pond, in the summer, and housed inside the Orangery in winter.

The Pond of the Swiss, begun in 1678 and completed in 1688, extends the Orangery Parterre over the Saint-Cyr road. It measures 682 metres long by 234 metres wide, or 16 hectares (twice the size of the *Place de la Concorde* in Paris).

The Hundred Steps

THE AVENUES AND GROVES

During the reign of Louis XIV, the gardens of Versailles comprised fifteen groves, areas hidden from view by hedgerows and enclosed by gates. They served as a counterpoint to the strict regularity of the general layout of the gardens, their décor and form varied greatly and they surprised visitors by their diversity. Most were created by Le Nôtre, but a few were later modified by Jules Hardouin-Mansart. These charming halls of greenery and fantasy havens abounded in water effects and sculptural décor. They served as a setting for festivities, dance, music, theatre or light meals. However, since they were difficult and expensive to maintain, certain groves rapidly deteriorated and closed as early as the 18th century. One of the most famous, the Maze Grove, was destroyed when the gardens were replanted in 1775-1776, and others such as the Baths of Apollo were reworked in the style of the English-Chinese gardens in vogue during the reign of Louis XVI and Marie-Antoinette. During the reign of Louis XVIII in the 19th century, the Royal Island was drained and became the King's Garden, planted with rare, exotic trees.

THE AVENUE OF BACCHUS AND SATURN

Parallel to the Royal Avenue, two main axes lead to the groves situated in the north and south of the gardens. To the south is the Avenue of Bacchus and Saturn interspersed by two fountains decorated in the middle with gilded lead statues, one of which was created by the Marsy brothers and the other by Girardon. Along with their counterparts to the north, these fountains symbolise the four seasons.

THE QUEEN'S GROVE

The Queen's Grove replaced the famous Maze Grove which illustrated thirty-nine of Aesop's Fables through the naturalistically painted lead fountains depicting animals at each of its cross-roads. Created in 1669, based on an idea by Charles Perrault, it was destroyed when the gardens were replanted in 1775-1776, and was replaced by the Queen's Grove. The present sculptural décor was installed at the end of the 19th century.

Medici Venus,
bronze cast
by the Keller brothers

Top right:
Bust of
a Roman woman
in the Queen's Grove

COLBERT, ORDERS
AND REGULATIONS
FOR THE BUILDINGS
OF VERSAILLES,
30 SEPTEMBER 1672

"In the gardens: as soon
as possible have Berthier,
the rock mason, set up two
or three workshops to restore
all the rockwork. [...]
Examine and repair
the rockwork such that it is fully
restored, using either cement
or brass wire: use that which
is the most solid.
Bring in the smelter,
and have him carefully inspect
all taps, valves, fittings
and all other copper works,
to renovate everything."

THE BALLROOM

Created by Le Nôtre between 1680 and 1683, the Ballroom is also known as the *Bosquet de Rocailles* due to the millstones and shells, brought from the African coast and Madagascar, beneath the cascading water. A floor was installed at the centre of the grove, which was used for dancing, an art form in which Louis XIV particularly distinguished himself. The musicians would be seated above the cascade and spectators would be able to sit on the grass-covered steps in the amphitheatre facing the cascade.

View of the ballroom with Armida crowning Renaud, by Jean Cotelle

Ceres,
by Théodon

Reaper,
after Poussin

Pomona,
after Poussin

THE DAUPHIN'S GROVE
AND THE CANDELABRA GROVE

The Dauphin's Grove and the Candelabra Grove, the restoration of which was completed in 2000, replace the former north and south quincunxes planted during the reign of Louis XVI. Each grove is decorated with terms commissioned by Superintendent Fouquet for his château at Vaux-Le-Vicomte and carved in Rome after models by Poussin. The sculptor Théodon completed this series of sculptures, dedicated to the seasons and mythological divinities, at the end of the 17th century.

THE SALLE DES MARRONNIERS

Arranged from 1680 to 1683, the *Salle des Marronniers* was then known as the *Salle des Antiques* or the *Galérie d'Eau*, and consisted of a central avenue lined with orange trees, trimmed yew trees, pools and fountains. Twenty-four classical statues once stood along the edges of the avenue.

Entirely reworked in 1704, this grove then became the *Salle des Marronniers*, adorned with eight classical busts and two statues. The two round pools at each end are the only remains of the original décor.

Meleager,
classical statue restored
in the 17th century

Septimus Severus,
17th-century
classical replica

THE KING'S GARDEN

The Mirror Pond used to be situated at one end of an expanse of water known as the Island of Love or Royal Island (1674) where models of warships were tested. Neglected during the Revolution, the Royal Island was drained in 1817 by the architect Dufour on Louis XVIII's orders, and replaced by the King's Garden. This enclosed English-style garden was planted with magnificent species, many of which disappeared during the storm of 1999. The Mirror Pond is all that remains of the original layout.

THE COLONNADE

The Colonnade, which Jules Hardouin-Mansart began building in 1685, replaced a grove created by Le Nôtre in 1679:
the Grove of the Springs. The peristyle measures thirty-two
metres in diameter; thirty-two marble columns of the Ionic
order, coupled with thirty-two Languedoc marble pilasters,
support the archways and a white marble cornice upon which
stand thirty-two urns. The triangular tympana between the
archways are decorated with bas-reliefs depicting children.
The keystones of the arches are adorned with heads of
nymphs and naiads. In the centre of the Colonnade, a circular
marble base serves as a pedestal for the famous group
executed by Girardon between 1678 and 1699: *The Rape of
Persephone by Pluto* (the original, now in reserve, has been
replaced by a copy).

*Bas-relief illustrating
the story of the abduction
of Persephone
by Pluto*

THE AVENUE OF FLORA AND CERES

Symmetrical to the Fountains of Bacchus and Saturn, the Fountains of Ceres and Flora symbolise summer and spring, respectively. Ceres, holding a sickle and surrounded by cupids, is lying on the ground strewn with ears of wheat, and is the work of the sculptor Regnaudin. Flora, semi-naked, is resting on a bed of flowers, surrounded by cupids weaving garlands. The sculptor Tuby created the latter group between 1672 and 1677.

THE BOSQUET DES DÔMES

This grove underwent considerable alterations and changed its name with its décor. Created by Le Nôtre in 1675, this grove was known as the Grove of Fame in 1677-1678 due to the statue of Fame then placed in the centre of the pool, sending forth a jet of water from her trumpet. The groups from the Baths of Apollo were placed there between 1684 and 1704, hence its name the Grove of the Baths of Apollo during that period. The grove took its current name from the two white marble domed pavilions which were built in 1677 by Jules Hardouin-Mansart and demolished in 1820.

The Bosquet des Dômes in 1688, by Simoneau Le Jeune

THE FOUNTAIN OF ENCELADUS

The Fountain of Enceladus was cast in lead by Gaspard Marsy between 1675 and 1677. The subject is taken from the story of the fall of the Titans, who were crushed beneath the rocks of Mount Olympus after they had attempted to scale it in defiance of Jupiter. The sculptor has represented the giant half-crushed beneath the rocks, fighting against death. The grove was restored between 1992 and 1998.

The Fountain of Enceladus at the start of the 17th century, French School

THE OBELISK GROVE

The Obelisk Fountain was built by Jules Hardouin-Mansart in 1704, on the site of the former Banqueting Hall or Council Chamber, created by Le Nôtre in 1671. The lead décor was then used to adorn the fountains in the garden of the Grand Trianon.

THE CHILDREN'S ISLAND

To the north of the gardens, between the *Rond Vert* (formerly the grove of the Water Theatre) and Star Grove (formerly the Water Mountain Grove), away from the busy avenues, a circular pool with a rock in the centre is concealed from view. This is the Children's Island, a masterpiece of spontaneity created by Hardy in 1710. On the rock, six naked children play with flowers while two others splash about in the water.

THE BATHS OF APOLLO

A grove, known as *Le Marais* or the Marsh, was created on this site during the reign of Louis XIV, between 1670 and 1673, under the influence of Madame de Montespan.

In 1704, Jules Hardouin-Mansart created a new grove for this site, which was to be the setting for the *Horses of the Sun* groups (the work of Guérin and the Marsy brothers) and the group depicting *Apollo Served by Nymphs* (by Girardon and Regnaudin). This ensemble was carved between 1664 and 1672 to decorate the famous Grotto of Thetis, and was transferred to the *Bosquet des Dômes* after the grotto was destroyed to build the north wing of the château.

Hardouin-Mansart therefore developed this site in order to highlight these particularly magnificent sculptures. They were placed on a base at the edge of a pool and sheltered by gilded lead canopies.

This situation lasted until 1776. At that time, a year after Louis XVI ordered the replanting of the park, Hubert Robert was commissioned to rework the existing grove. His new grove, completed in 1778, was in the style of the then fashionable English-Chinese gardens, and it is this grove that we see today.

The Horses of the Sun,
by the Marsy brothers

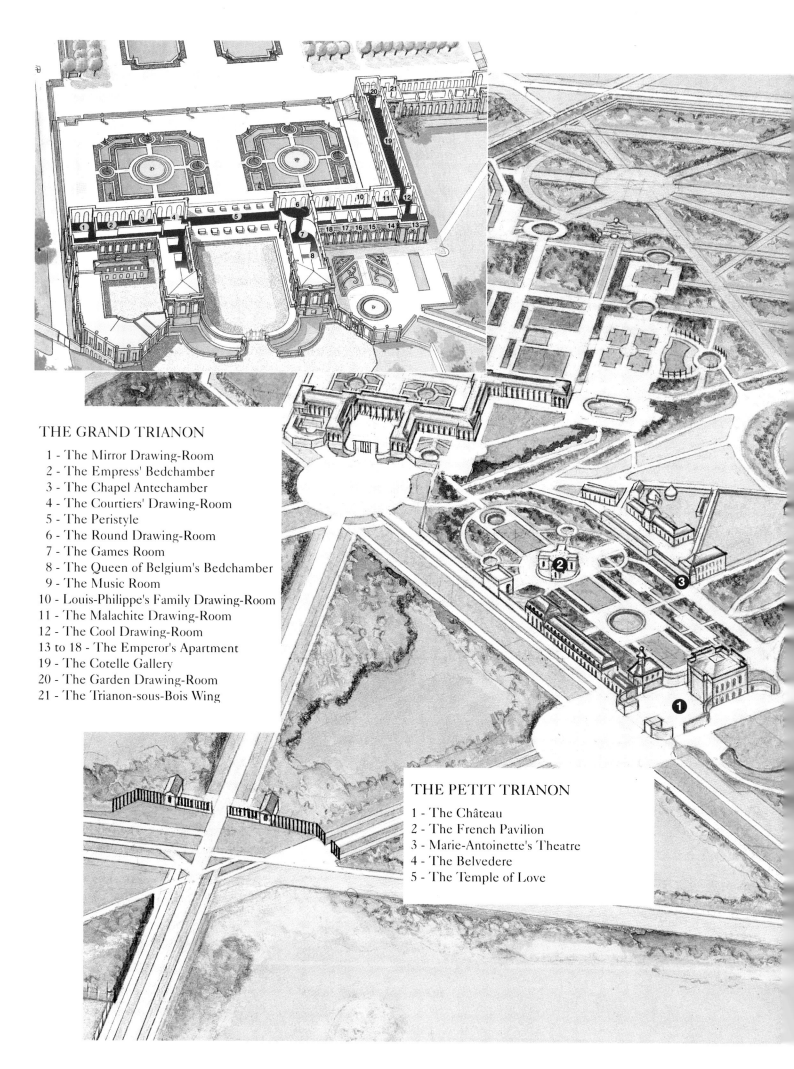

THE GRAND TRIANON

1 - The Mirror Drawing-Room
2 - The Empress' Bedchamber
3 - The Chapel Antechamber
4 - The Courtiers' Drawing-Room
5 - The Peristyle
6 - The Round Drawing-Room
7 - The Games Room
8 - The Queen of Belgium's Bedchamber
9 - The Music Room
10 - Louis-Philippe's Family Drawing-Room
11 - The Malachite Drawing-Room
12 - The Cool Drawing-Room
13 to 18 - The Emperor's Apartment
19 - The Cotelle Gallery
20 - The Garden Drawing-Room
21 - The Trianon-sous-Bois Wing

THE PETIT TRIANON

1 - The Château
2 - The French Pavilion
3 - Marie-Antoinette's Theatre
4 - The Belvedere
5 - The Temple of Love

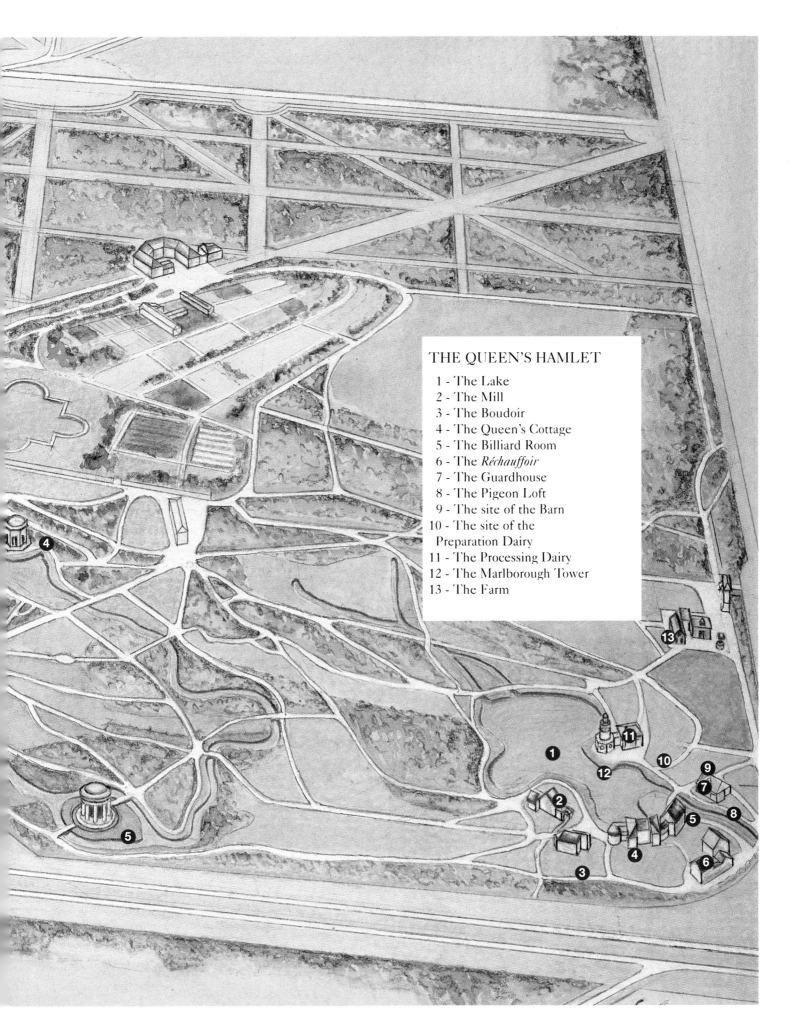

THE QUEEN'S HAMLET

1 - The Lake
2 - The Mill
3 - The Boudoir
4 - The Queen's Cottage
5 - The Billiard Room
6 - The *Réchauffoir*
7 - The Guardhouse
8 - The Pigeon Loft
9 - The site of the Barn
10 - The site of the
Preparation Dairy
11 - The Processing Dairy
12 - The Marlborough Tower
13 - The Farm

THE GRAND TRIANON

In 1670, Louis XIV ordered the architect Le Vau to construct a building that would become known as the "Porcelain Trianon", on the site of the former village of Trianon. The walls were completely lined with blue and white delft tiles. Destroyed in 1687, it was replaced the following year by the "Marble Trianon", which exists today, the work of Jules Hardouin-Mansart.

The Grand Trianon was reserved for concerts, festivities and light meals, and was a place of rest, a private area where Louis XIV could invite the ladies of the Court.

The gardens of Trianon were dedicated to flowers, with many varieties chosen not only for their colour but also for their perfume. In a letter dated 8 August 1689, Madame de Maintenon wrote: "The tuberose plants forced us to leave Trianon every night, much too early; but most of the men and women fell ill from too much perfume…"

THE EMPRESS' BEDCHAMBER

This bedchamber was occupied by Empress Marie-Louise and then by Queen Marie-Amélie. The furniture is that used by the sovereigns. The bed brought from the Tuileries for Marie-Amélie was commissioned by Napoleon I from Jacob in 1809.

THE MIRROR DRAWING-ROOM

DUC DE SAINT-SIMON

"During a visit to Trianon, the princesses (the Princesse de Conty Douairière, the Duchesse de Bourbon-Condé, and the Duchesse de Chartres), who were staying there and who were young, would go out walking together at night and amuse themselves with firecrackers.

One night, either through the mischief of the two elder princesses, or through carelessness, they let one off beneath the windows of Monsieur who awoke and found it most unpleasant; he made his complaints known to the King who apologised profusely, scolded the princesses, and took great trouble to appease him."

The mirror décor dates from the reign of Louis XIV in 1706. Some of the furniture belonged to Empress Marie-Louise who used this room as her State Cabinet. Two small stone temples given to Napoleon I by Charles IV, King of Spain, are situated on the two console tables.

THE COURTIERS' DRAWING-ROOM

This room served as the Courtiers' Antechamber during the reign of Louis XIV, and later became known as the Princes'Drawing-Room during the 18th century. In 1805, it served as the antechamber of Madame Mère, and in 1810 became the dining-room of the Emperor and Empress' suite. In 1836, it was the drawing-room of Queen Marie-Amélie's ushers.

The large table made by Félix Rémond in 1823 consists of a teak table-top measuring 2.77 m in diameter, on an elm base. The painting above the fireplace is a Mignard replica by Delutel portraying the eldest son of Louis XIV and his family.

L'ILLUSTRATION,
4 OCTOBER 1873

"We do not need to inform our readers that the trial of Maréchal Bazaine will take place in the vestibule of the Grand Trianon, the château so dear to King Louis-Philippe. All of the necessary arrangements have already been made, and the large vestibule has been altered so as to fulfil all the requirements of its temporary new purpose."

THE PERISTYLE

The Peristyle was based on an idea by the architect Robert de Cotte, approved by Louis XIV who used it for light meals and suppers. Napoleon found this passageway impractical since it was exposed to the wind and, in 1810, had it closed with movable glass partitions, which were finally taken down in 1910.

THE ROUND DRAWING-ROOM

This vestibule used to lead to the King's Apartment during the *Ancien Régime*. In the 19th century, it served as the Ushers'Drawing-Room. The paintings date from the reign of Louis XIV: *Juno and Thetis* and *The Abduction of Oreithyia by Boreas*, by François Verdier, and *Flowers and Fruit of America*, by François Desportes, above the door.

THE MALACHITE DRAWING-ROOM

This drawing-room takes its name from the stone slabs given to Napoleon by Czar Alexander I, and fashioned in 1809 by Jacob Desmalter. This was the Emperor's State Drawing-Room.

LOUIS-PHILIPPE'S FAMILY DRAWING-ROOM

Louis-Philippe connected two rooms known as the Games Antechamber and the Bedchamber during the reign of the Sun King, and as the Drawing-Room of the High Officers and the Princes' Drawing-Room during the Empire. The family of the citizen king would gather here in the evening.

MARQUIS DE SOUCHES,
26 APRIL 1694

"On the 28th, the King went to Trianon for a few days, where he invited everyone to come and pay court to him at any time, like at Versailles, and even permitted a few ladies to dine with the princesses each day..."

THE QUEEN OF BELGIUM'S BEDCHAMBER

In 1845, Louis-Philippe had the former dining-room of Louis XV transformed into a bedchamber for his daughter Louise-Marie d'Orléans who, in 1832, had married Leopold I of Saxe-Coburg, King of Belgium. The furniture was brought here from the Tuileries, the bed once belonged to Empress Joséphine, and two chests of drawers and a console table in the style of Boulle were also added.

*Console table
in the style
of Boulle*

DUC DE SAINT-SIMON
"On Tuesday
17 December 1697,
the court went
to Trianon at 4 o'clock,
where we amused
ourselves until the arrival
of the King and Queen
of England. The King led
them into a gallery where
we went up to the concert
hall from Madame
de Maintenon's rooms.
The rest of the court was
below in the auditorium.
Des Touches' *Opéra d'Yssé*
was beautifully
performed."

THE EMPEROR'S TOPOGRAPHICAL CABINET

This room was where the apartment of Madame de Maintenon began, and has been recreated as it was when Napoleon I made it into his private apartment. It was known as the Drawing-Room of the Springs during the reign of Louis XIV because of the grove onto which it looked.

MARQUIS DE SOUCHES,
23 JULY 1685
"On the 23rd of July,
we celebrated at Versailles
the wedding of
the Duc de Bourbon with
Mlle de Nantes [...] at 10 o'clock,
the King landed at the foot
of Trianon, and having come up
through the garden,
a wonderful supper was laid
out on four different tables;
it was served in the four rooms
which look onto the garden,
all lit by a large number
of crystal chandeliers."

THE EMPEROR'S BEDCHAMBER

The Empire décor of this room has been restored, with its fawn moiré hangings decorated with lilac and silver, woven in Lyon, delivered for Joséphine in 1807, and reused for Napoleon at Trianon in 1809.

THE GAMES ROOM

Until 1703, this and the following room served as a theatre auditorium which could be converted into a ballroom, and which also contained a gallery for the king.

Louis XIV then had the rooms transformed into a new apartment. During the reign of Louis XV, it comprised a games room, a dining-room, and a buffet room.

QUEEN HORTENSE,
25 DECEMBER 1809

"He [the Emperor] went to Trianon and asked us [Hortense and Joséphine] to come and visit. I went along with my mother. This meeting was very touching. The Emperor wanted her to stay for dinner. As usual he was seated in front of her. Seemingly nothing had changed. The Queen of Naples and I were alone. The room was very quiet. My mother was unable to eat a thing and I could tell she was on the verge of fainting. The Emperor wiped his eyes two or three times without saying a word and we left immediately after dinner."

THE COTELLE GALLERY

The gallery opens onto the south through its eleven windows which let in a great deal of light, with only five windows on the northern side to protect it from the harshness of winter. Twenty-four paintings were commissioned at the end of 1687 (including twenty-one by the painter Jean Cotelle), portraying the fountains and groves of Versailles. This collection provides a valuable account of the appearance of the gardens of Versailles and Trianon in the 17th century. Settees were originally placed in the alcoves, but Louis-Philippe had them replaced by two Languedoc marble *rafraîchissoirs* situated in the buffet room during the reign of Louis XV. The peace treaty with Hungary was signed here on 4 June 1920, which finally brought the First World War to an end.

View of the Trianon Parterres with Flora and Zephyr, by Jean Cotelle

THE GARDEN DRAWING-ROOM

Built on the site of the former Perfume Cabinet of the Porcelain Trianon, during the reign of Louis XIV, the Garden Drawing-Room housed a bar-billiard table, followed by a billiard table in the 18th century. Six large windows provide a prime view of the gardens, hence its name.

Exterior view of the Garden Drawing-Room

THE TRIANON-SOUS-BOIS WING

Reserved for the Head of State since the restoration of the Grand Trianon in 1967, this wing has recently opened its doors to the public. Trianon-sous-Bois was occupied during the reign of Louis XIV, by his sister-in-law, Princess Palatine and her children and, under Louis-Philippe, by the King's youngest son.

THE CHAPEL

It was Louis-Philippe who transformed Louis XIV's former billiard room into a chapel. The wedding of his second daughter, Princess Marie, to Duke Alexander of Würtemberg was held here on 17 October 1837. The columns on either side of the altar were originally from the *Bosquet des Dômes*, and the stained-glass window was commissioned from the Sèvres works, depicting *The Assumption of the Virgin* in the style of Pierre-Paul Prud'hon.

THE GENERAL'S STUDY

General De Gaulle's study was one of the rooms restored between 1962 and 1967 to serve as a residence for the presidents of the French Republic when the Grand Trianon became the State residence for France's visitors.

THE PETIT TRIANON

At the suggestion of Madame de Pompadour, the Petit Trianon was created in 1768, supplementing the prestigious botanical garden, the Menagerie and the French Pavilion. The architect Gabriel thus designed the square neoclassical building, each room of which offered a new view over the gardens. However, the Petit Trianon is essentially dedicated to the memory of Marie-Antoinette. In 1774, the first year of his reign, Louis XVI gave his Queen this dwelling as a gift so that she would be able to make a life for herself here away from the Court. Louis XV's botanical garden gave way to an "English-Chinese" garden designed by Richard Mique. The Temple of Love, the Belvedere and the Chinese ring game (a type of merry-go-round) were then added, followed by the Queen's theatre in 1780.

THE RECEPTION ROOM

Reserved for games, conversation and music, this room with its sober décor provides an accurate impression of the pursuit of happiness specific to the 18th century. The paintings above the doors, inspired by Ovid's *Metamorphosis*, reveal the importance of flowers at Trianon: *Clytia Turned into a Sunflower* and *Apollo and Hyacinth*, by Nicolas-René Jollain; *Adonis Turned into an Anemone* and *Narcissus Turned into a Flower of the Same Name*, by Nicolas-Bernard Lépicié. The ostrich egg on the pedestal table is from the collections of Madame Adélaïde, Louis XV's daughter.

Marie-Antoinette holding a rose,
by Elisabeth Vigée-Lebrun

MADAME CAMPAN,
CHIEF CHAMBERMAID
TO MARIE-ANTOINETTE
"She [Marie-Antoinette] took
a liking to her retreat at Trianon;
she would go there alone,
followed by a footman,
but would find there a service
ready to welcome her: a caretaker
and his wife, who then served
as a chambermaid."

THE FRENCH PAVILION

Built by Gabriel in 1750, the French Pavilion was a place of rest for Louis XV during his visits to the new botanical garden and the new menagerie at Trianon. The building is in the shape of a cross. Four cabinets are annexed to a vast circular drawing-room: a boudoir, a *réchauffoir*, a kitchen, and a dressing-room.

MARIE-ANTOINETTE'S THEATRE

Marie-Antoinette loved playing herself in performances which would have only her closest relations as the audience. She therefore wished to have her own theatre close to the Petit Trianon where she often stayed. Her architect, Richard Mique, built the theatre between 1778 and 1780. The plainness of the exterior revealed nothing of the sumptuous interior décor. The stage, used for operas, seems almost disproportionate relative to the modest size of the auditorium; however, this theatre was exclusively reserved for a limited audience. The blue and gold décor uses modest materials such as pasteboard for the sculptures or wood painted in false veined white marble. The original ceiling, which has now disappeared, was the work of Lagrenée, depicting Apollo, the Muses and the Graces, and has been replaced by a copy.

MADAME CAMPAN,
CHIEF CHAMBERMAID
TO MARIE-ANTOINETTE

"*La Gageure imprévue* was one of the plays performed at Trianon. The Queen played the role of Gotte, Madame Elisabeth, the young person, and the Comte d'Artois one of the male roles. The role of Colette in *Le Devin de village* was played extremely well by the Queen. *Le Roi et le Fermier, Rose et Colas, Le Sorcier, L'Anglais à Bordeaux, On ne s'avise jamais de tout,* and *Le Barbier de Séville* etc. were also performed over the next few years."

THE BELVEDERE

In 1777, this neoclassical pavilion was erected by Richard Mique on a mound commanding a view over the lake. The sculptures on the pediments depict rustic pleasures and the bas-reliefs symbolise the four seasons. The interior is paved with marble mosaic. The walls are decorated with arabesques painted by Le Riche, and the sky with passing clouds and cupids, painted on the dome, is the work of Lagrenée.

Top:
Illumination of the Belvedere
and the rock on 3 August 1781,
in honour of Joseph II,
brother of Marie-Antoinette,
by L.-C. Châtelet

THE TEMPLE OF LOVE

In 1778, Richard Mique built the "Temple of Love", visible from the Queen's bedchamber at the Petit Trianon, with a sculpture by Bouchardon at its centre: *Cupid Carving His Bow*, which is a replica by the artist himself of the original work now in the Louvre Museum.

Cupid Carving His Bow from Hercules' Club, by Bouchardon (replica of the original now in the Louvre Museum)

THE QUEEN'S HAMLET

This hamlet, built by Mique between 1783 and 1785, was made up of twelve houses, ten of which still stand. It was not the first "fairytale hamlet" to have been built in the 18th century: Madame de Lamballe had her own hamlet at Rambouillet and the Condés had also had one built at Chantilly. The exteriors had every semblance of a genuine hamlet inhabited by simple folk, which contrasted with the sophisticated interior décor of the houses.

The Queen's Cottage stands opposite an artificial lake. On the left, a small bridge leads to the guardhouse and the pigeon loft. All that is left of the barn (which also served as a ballroom) and the preparation dairy are a few foundations.

A real farm, restored in 1993, was situated away from the hamlet: "Gardens were planted, fields were tilled, trees were pruned, and the fruit was picked. From her house, the Queen could see the donkey bringing the grain to the mill…" (Pierre de Nolhac).

The water mill, restored in 1994

The Queen's Cottage actually consists
of two buildings linked by a gallery:
to the left is the billiard room
and to the right the Queen's Cottage itself.
Behind is the "Réchauffoir",
currently being restored

The Marlborough Tower,
at the foot of which is a fishery

CRÉDITS PHOTOGRAPHIQUES

P. 16 : RMN ; p. 18 : RMN/Blot ; p. 19 : RMN/Blot ; p. 20 : Art Lys/Girard ; p. 21 : RMN/Arnaudet ; p. 22 : RMN/Blot ; p. 23 : RMN ; p. 24 : RMN/Blot ; p. 25 : RMN/Blot ; p. 26 : RMN/Blot ; p. 27 : RMN/Blot ; p. 28 : Art Lys/Février ; p. 29 : RMN/Bréjat ; p. 30 : RMN/Blot ; p. 31 : RMN/Blot ; p. 32 : RMN ; p. 33 : RMN/Blot ; p. 34 : RMN/Arnaudet/Lewandowski ; p. 36 : RMN/Blot ; p. 37 : RMN/Bréjat ; p. 38 : RMN ; p. 39 : RMN/Bréjat ; p. 40 : RMN/Bréjat ; p. 41 : RMN/Bréjat ; p. 42 : RMN/Blot ; p. 43 : RMN/Bréjat ; p. 44 : RMN/Bréjat ; p. 46 : RMN/Arnaudet ; p. 47 : RMN/Blot/Lewandowski ; p. 48 : RMN/Blot ; p. 49 : RMN/Blot ; p. 50 : RMN/Blot/Lewandowski ; p. 52 : RMN/Bréjat ; p. 53 : Art Lys/Février ; p. 54 : RMN/Arnaudet ; p. 55 : RMN/Bréjat ; p. 56 : RMN ; p. 58 : RMN/Blot ; p. 59 : RMN/Blot/Jean ; p. 60 : RMN/Bréjat ; p. 62 : RMN/Bernard ; p. 63 : RMN ; p. 64 : RMN/Blot ; p. 65 : RMN/Blot ; p. 66 : RMN ; p. 67 : RMN/Blot ; p. 68 : RMN/Arnaudet ; p. 69 : RMN/Blot ; p. 70 : RMN ; p. 71 : RMN/Blot, RMN ; p. 72 : RMN/Bréjat ; p. 73 : RMN/Peter Willi ; p. 74 : RMN ; p. 75 : RMN/Jean/Marbœuf ; p. 76 : RMN/Arnaudet/Blot ; p. 77 : Art Lys/Varga ; p. 78 : RMN/Bréjat ; p. 79 : RMN/Blot ; p. 80 : Art Lys/Varga ; p. 82 : Art Lys/Février ; p. 83 : RMN/Lewandowski ; p. 84 : RMN/Bréjat ; p. 85 : RMN/Bréjat ; p. 86 : RMN/Blot ; p. 87 : RMN/Blot, RMN/Bernard ; p. 88 : Art Lys/Burnier, RMN/Bernard ; p. 89 : Art Lys/Burnier ; p. 90 : RMN/Bréjat ; p. 91 : RMN/Bréjat ; p. 92 : RMN/Blot ; p. 93 : Art Lys/Varga ; p. 94 : RMN/Bréjat, RMN/Blot ; p. 95 : RMN/Lewandowski ; p. 96 : RMN/Blot ; p. 97 : RMN/Blot, RMN/Arnaudet/Lewandowski ; p. 98 : RMN ; p. 99 : Art Lys/Varga ; p. 100 : RMN/Bréjat ; p. 101 : RMN/Bréjat ; p. 102 : RMN/Bréjat ; p. 103 : RMN/Bréjat, RMN/Blot ; p. 104 : RMN/Blot, RMN/Bréjat ; p. 105 : RMN/Bréjat, RMN/Blot ; p. 106 : RMN/Arnaudet/Lewandowski ; p. 107 : RMN/Lewandowski ; p. 108 : RMN/Blot, RMN/Arnaudet ; p. 109 : RMN ; p. 110 : RMN/Arnaudet ; p. 111 : RMN/Blot ; p. 112 : RMN/Blot ; p. 113 : RMN/Arnaudet ; p. 114 : Art Lys/Girard ; p. 116 : Art Lys/Février ; p. 117 : RMN/Arnaudet, Art Lys/Girard ; p. 118 : Art Lys/Schmitt ; p. 119 : RMN/Bréjat ; p. 120 : Art Lys/Février ; p. 122 : RMN/Bréjat ; p. 123 : Art Lys/Février ; p. 124 : Art Lys/Février ; p. 125 : RMN/Bréjat ; p. 126 : Art Lys/Février ; p. 127 : Art Lys/Février, RMN/Bréjat ; p. 128 : RMN/Arnaudet ; p. 129 : RMN/Bréjat ; p. 130 : Art Lys/Schmitt, Art Lys/Février ; p. 131 : Art Lys/Février ; p. 132 : Art Lys/Girard, RMN/Blot, p. 133 : RMN/Blot, Art Lys/Burnier, Art Lys/Girard ; p. 134 : RMN/Bréjat, Art Lys/Girard ; p. 135 : RMN/Bréjat ; p. 136 : RMN/Arnaudet ; p. 137 : RMN/Bréjat ; p. 138 : Art Lys/Février ; p. 139 : Art Lys/Février ; p. 140 : RMN/Bréjat, RMN ; p. 141 : Art Lys/Février ; p. 142 : Art Lys/Février ; p. 143 : RMN/Arnaudet/Blot, Art Lys/Girard ; p. 144 : Art Lys/Girard, RMN/Blot, Art Lys/Février ; p. 145 : Art Lys/Girard, Art Lys/Février ; p. 146 : Art Lys/Février, RMN/Blot ; p. 147 : Art Lys/Girard ; p. 148 : Art Lys/Février ; p. 149 : Art Lys/Girard ; p. 150 : RMN/Blot ; p. 151 : Art Lys/Février ; p. 152 : Art Lys/Girard ; p. 153 : Art Lys/Girard ; p. 154 : Art Lys/Février ; p. 155 : Art Lys/Février ; p. 158 : RMN/Blot ; p. 159 : Art Lys/Girard ; p. 160 : RMN/Blot ; p. 161 : RMN/Blot ; p. 162 : RMN/Bréjat ; p. 163 : RMN/Bréjat ; p. 164 : RMN/Blot ; p. 165 : RMN/Blot, RMN/Bréjat ; p. 166 : RMN/Bréjat ; p. 167 : RMN/Bréjat ; p. 168 : RMN/Bréjat ; p. 170 : RMN/Blot ; p. 171 : RMN/Blot ; p. 172 : RMN/Blot ; p. 173 : RMN/Blot ; p. 174 : RMN/Bréjat ; p. 175 : RMN/Bréjat ; p. 176 : RMN/Bréjat ; p. 177 : RMN/Bréjat ; p. 178 : RMN/Blot ; p. 179 : RMN ; p. 180 : RMN/Blot ; p. 181 : RMN/Blot ; p. 182 : RMN ; p. 183 : Art Lys/Février ; p. 184 : RMN/Arnaudet, Art Lys/Girard ; p. 185 : Art Lys/Girard, RMN/Blot ; p. 186 : Art Lys/Burnier ; p. 188 : Art Lys/Burnier ; p. 190 : RMN/Blot.

Achevé d'imprimer
le 30 janvier 2001
sur les Presses de Bretagne, Rennes

Dépôt légal Février 2001